A Guide to Scaffold Use in the Construction Industry

Small Business Safety Management Series

U.S. Department of Labor
Elaine L. Chao, Secretary

Occupational Safety and Health Administration
John L. Henshaw, Assistant Secretary

OSHA 3150
2002 (Revised)

The Occupational Safety and Health Act of 1970 charges the Occupational Safety and Health Administration (OSHA) with protecting all working men and women across the United States. To do so, the agency sets federal standards[1] for general industry, construction, and shipyard employment. OSHA also promotes a variety of voluntary programs that strive to form partnerships with businesses, labor, and other groups to help employers provide safer and more healthful workplaces for employees. Some of the agency's voluntary initiatives include safety and health management programs, the Voluntary Protection Programs, consultation assistance, and training and education programs and grants. For more information on these outreach efforts, see page 12 of this booklet.

The agency's recent rule, *Safety Standards for Scaffolds Use in the Construction Industry* rule aims to protect workers using scaffolding in construction work. Scaffolding hazards continue to rank high on the list of the most frequently cited standards in the construction industry. Scaffold-related fatalities account for a significant number of fatalities in the construction workplace. This booklet addresses some of the most common questions about OSHA's scaffold standard. It is all part of the agency's effort to provide guidance to employers who need help in complying with OSHA's standards to protect the working men and women across the nation.

This booklet is organized in a question and answer format to highlight pertinent information that employers and employees need to know. The subjects addressed in each question follow the basic organization of the standard. In addition, each answer references the regulatory text where that particular information can be located. These references appear at the end of each answer in boldface type.

An appendix also includes an alphabetical index to the standard for quick reference.

It is important to note that the question and answer section of this booklet simply provides an *overview* of the standard. For compliance with **all** of the regulation's requirements, refer to the regulatory text or *Title 29 of the Code Federal Regulations* (*CFR*) Part 1926, Subpart L.

---

[1] *Section 18(b) of **The Occupational Safety and Health Act of 1970**, P.L. 91-596, encourages states to develop and operate, under OSHA guidance, their own job safety and health plans. An OSHA-approved state plan must have safety and health requirements at least as effective as those of Federal OSHA and must adopt comparable state standards within 6 months of promulgation of federal standards.*

What are the highlights of the scaffolding standard?

OSHA's scaffolding standard has several key provisions:

- Fall protection or fall arrest systems—Each employee more than 10 feet above a lower level shall be protected from falls by guardrails or a fall arrest system, except those on single-point and two-point adjustable suspension scaffolds. Each employee on a single-point and two-point adjustable suspended scaffold shall be protected by both a personal fall arrest system and a guardrail. **1926.451(g)(1)**

- Guardrail height—The height of the toprail for scaffolds manufactured and placed in service after January 1, 2000 must be between 38 inches (0.9 meters) and 45 inches (1.2 meters). The height of the toprail for scaffolds manufactured and placed in service before January 1, 2000 can be between 36 inches (0.9 meters) and 45 inches (1.2 meters). **1926.451(g)(4)(ii)**

- Crossbracing—When the crosspoint of crossbracing is used as a toprail, it must be between 38 inches (0.97 m) and 48 inches (1.3 meters) above the work platform. **1926.451(g)(4)(xv)**

- Midrails— Midrails must be installed approximately halfway between the toprail and the platform surface. When a crosspoint of crossbracing is used as a midrail, it must be between 20 inches (0.5 meters) and 30 inches (0.8 m) above the work platform. **1926.451(g)(4)**

- Footings—Support scaffold footings shall be level and capable of supporting the loaded scaffold. The legs, poles, frames, and uprights shall bear on base plates and mud sills. **1926.451(c)(2)**

- Platforms—Supported scaffold platforms shall be fully planked or decked. **1926.451(b)**

- Guying ties, and braces—Supported scaffolds with a height-to-base of more than 4:1 shall be restained from tipping by guying, tying, bracing, or the equivalent. **1926.451(c)(1)**

- Capacity—Scaffolds and scaffold components must support at least 4 times the maximum intended load. Suspension scaffold rigging must at least 6 times the intended load. **1926.451(a)(1) and (3)**

- Training—Employers must train each employee who works on a scaffold on the hazards and the procedures to control the hazards. **1926.454**

- Inspections—Before each work shift and after any occurrence that could affect the structural integrity, a competent person must inspect the scaffold and scaffold components for visible defects. **1926.451(f)(3)**

- Erecting and Dismantling—When erecting and dismantling supported scaffolds, a competent person[2] must determine the feasibility of providing a safe means of access and fall protection for these operations. **1926.451(e)(9) & (g)(2)**

When is a competent person required for scaffolding?

OSHA's scaffolding standard defines a competent person as "one who is capable of identifying existing and predictable hazards in the surroundings or working conditions, which are unsanitary, hazardous to employees, and who has authorization to take prompt corrective measures to eliminate them."

The standard requires a competent person to perform the following duties under these circumstances:

- *In General:*
  - To select and direct employees who erect, dismantle, move, or alter scaffolds. **1926.451(f)(7)**
  - To determine if it is safe for employees to work on or from a scaffold during storms or high winds and to ensure that a personal fall arrest system or wind screens protect these employees. (Note: Windscreens should not be used unless the scaffold is secured against the anticipated wind forces imposed.) **1926.451(f)(12)**

- *For Training:*
  - To train employees involved in erecting, disassembling, moving, operating, repairing, maintaining, or inspecting scaffolds to recognize associated work hazards. **1926.454(b)**

- *For Inspections:*
  - To inspect scaffolds and scaffold components for visible defects before each work shift and after any occurrence which could affect the structural integrity and to authorize prompt corrective actions. **1926.451(f)(3)**

---

[2] *See the standard's requirements for and definition of a competent person in the next question.*

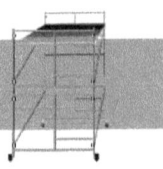

- To inspect ropes on suspended scaffolds prior to each workshift and after every occurrence which could affect the structural integrity and to authorize prompt corrective actions. **1926.451(d)(10)**
- To inspect manila or plastic (or other synthetic) rope being used for toprails or midrails. **1926.451(g)(4)(xiv)**

• *For Suspension Scaffolds:*
- To evaluate direct connections to support the load. 1926.451 (d)(3)(i)
- To evaluate the need to secure two-point and multi-point scaffolds to prevent swaying. **1926.451(d)(18)**

• *For Erectors and Dismantlers:*
- To determine the feasibility and safety of providing fall protection and access. **1926.451(e)(9) and 1926.451(g)(2)**
- To train erectors and dismantlers (effective September 2, 1997) to recognize associated work hazards. **1926.454(b)**

• *For Scaffold Components:*
- To determine if a scaffold will be structurally sound when intermixing components from different manufacturers. **1926.451(b)(10)**
- To determine if galvanic action has affected the capacity when using components of dissimilar metals. **1926.451(b)(11)**

When is a qualified person required for scaffolding?

The standard defines a qualified person as "one who—by possession of a recognized degree, certificate, or professional standing, or who by extensive knowledge, training, and experience—has successfully demonstrated his/her ability to solve or resolve problems related to the subject matter, the work, or the project."

The qualified person must perform the following duties in these circumstances:

• *In General:*
- To design and load scaffolds in accordance with that design. **1926.451(a)(6)**

• *For Training:*
- To train employees working on the scaffolds to recognize the associated hazards and understand procedures to control or minimize those hazards. **1926.454(a)**

• *For Suspension Scaffolds:*
- To design the rigging for single-point adjustable suspension scaffolds. **1926.452(o)(2)(i)**
- To design platforms on two-point adjustable suspension types that are less than 36 inches (0.9 m) wide to prevent instability. **1926.452(p)(1)**
- To make swaged attachments or spliced eyes on wire suspension ropes. **1926.451(d)(11)**

• *For Components and Design:*
- To design scaffold components construction in accordance with the design. **1926.451(a)(6)**

When is an engineer required?

The standard requires a registered professional engineer to perform the following duties in these circumstances:

• *For Suspension Scaffolds:*
- To design the direct connections of masons' multi-point adjustable suspension scaffolds. **1926.451(d)(3)(i)**

• *For Design:*
- To design scaffolds that are to be moved when employees are on them. **1926.451(f)(5)**
- To design pole scaffolds over 60 feet (18.3 meters) in height. **1926.452(a)(10)**
- To design tube and coupler scaffolds over 125 feet (38 meters) in height. **1926.452(b)(10)**
- To design fabricated frame scaffolds over 125 feet (38 meters) in height above their base plates. **1926.452(c)(6)**
- To design brackets on fabricated frame scaffolds used to support cantilevered loads in addition to workers. **1926.452(c)(5)**
- To design outrigger scaffolds and scaffold components. **1926.452(i)(8)**

What other standards apply to scaffolds?

29 CFR contains other standards that apply to construction work such as the responsibility to initiate and maintain programs (**1926.29(b)(1)**); exposures to dusts and chemicals (**1926.33, .55, .59, .62, and .1101**); hand and power tools (**1926.300 - .307**); electrical (**1926.300 - .449**); personal fall arrest systems (**1926.502**); and ladders (**1926.1050 - .1060**).

Capacity

What are the capacity requirements for all scaffolds?

Each scaffold and scaffold component must support without failure its own weight and at least four times the maximum intended load applied or transmitted to it. **1926.451(a)(1)**

A qualified person must design the scaffolds, which are loaded in accordance with that design. **1926.451(a)(6)**

Scaffolds and scaffold components must not be loaded in excess of their maximum intended loads or rated capacities, whichever is less. **1926.451(f)(1)**

Load carrying timber members should be a minimum of 1,500 lb-f/in^2 construction grade lumber. **Appendix A (1)(a)**

Scaffold Platform Construction

What are scaffold platform construction requirements?

Each platform must be planked and decked as fully as possible with the space between the platform and uprights not more than 1 inch (2.5 centimeters) wide. The space must not exceed 9 inches (24.1 centimetersm) when side brackets or odd-shaped structures result in a wider opening between the platform and the uprights. **1926.451(b)(1)**

What are the requirements for scaffold planking?

Scaffold planking must be able to support, without failure, its own weight and at least four times the intended load. **1926.451(a)(1)**

Solid sawn wood, fabricated planks, and fabricated platforms may be used as scaffold planks following the recommendations by the manufacturer or a lumber grading association or inspection agency. **Appendix A (1)(b) and (c)**

Tables showing maximum permissible spans, rated load capacity, and nominal thickness are in **Appendix A (1)(b) & (c)** of the standard.

What is the maximum deflection of a platform?

The platform must not deflect more than 1/60 of the span when loaded. **1926.451(f)(16)**

Are there requirements for work on platforms cluttered with debris?

The standard prohibits work on platforms cluttered with debris. **1926.451(f)(13)**

How wide does the work area need to be on scaffolding?

Each scaffold platform and walkway must be at least 18 inches (46 centimeters) wide. When the work area is less than 18 inches (46 centimeters) wide, guardrails and/or personal fall arrest systems must be used. **1926.451(b)(2)**

Are guardrails required on all open sides of scaffolding?

The standard requires employers to protect each employee on a scaffold more than 10 feet (3.1 m) above a lower level from falling to that lower level. **1926.451(g)(1)**

To ensure adequate protection, install guardrails along all open sides and ends before releasing the scaffold for use by employees, other than the erection and dismantling crews. **1926.451(g)(4)**

Guardrails are not required, however,
- When the front end of all platforms are less than 14 inches (36 centimeters) from the face of the work; **1926.451(b)(3)**

- When outrigger scaffolds are 3 inches (8 centimeters) or less from the front edge; **1926.451(b)(3)(I)**

- When employees are plastering and lathing 18 inches (46 centimeters) or less from the front edge. **1926.451(b)(3)(ii)**

What materials are unacceptable for guardrails?

Steel or plastic banding must not be used as a toprail or a midrail. **1926.451(g)(4)(xiii)**

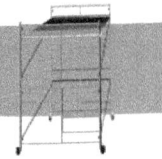

Criteria for Supported Scaffolds

What are supported scaffolds?

Supported scaffolds are platforms supported by legs, outrigger beams, brackets, poles, uprights, posts, frames, or similar rigid support. **1926.451(b)**

The structural members, poles, legs, posts, frames, and uprights, must be plumb and braced to prevent swaying and displacement. **1926.451(c)(3)**

Do employees working on supported scaffolds need to be trained?

All employees must be trained by a qualified person to recognize the hazards associated with the type of scaffold being used and how to control or minimize those hazards. The training must include fall hazards, falling object hazards, electrical hazards, proper use of the scaffold, and handling of materials. **1926.454(a)**

When do supported scaffolds need to be restrained from tipping?

Supported scaffolds with a height to base width ratio of more than 4:1 must be restrained by guying, tying, bracing, or an equivalent means. **1926.451(c)(1)**

How can one prevent supported scaffolding from tipping?

Either the manufacturers' recommendation or the following placements must be used for guys, ties, and braces:

- Install guys, ties, or braces at the closest horizontal member to the 4:1 height and repeat vertically with the top restraint no further than the 4:1 height from the top.

- Vertically—every 20 feet (6.1 meters) or less for scaffolds less than three feet (0.91 meters) wide; every 26 feet (7.9 meters) or less for scaffolds more than three feet (0.91 meters) wide.

- Horizontally—at each end; at intervals not to exceed 30 feet (9.1 meters) from one end. **1926.451(c)(1)**

What are the footing and foundation requirements for supported scaffolds?

Supported scaffolds' poles, legs, posts, frames, and uprights must bear on base plates and mud sills, or other adequate firm foundation. **1926.451(c)(2)(i) and (ii)**

May forklifts, front-end loaders, or similar equipment support platforms?

Forklifts can support platforms only when the entire platform is attached to the fork and the forklift does not move horizontally when workers are on the platform. **1926.451(c)(2)(v)**

Front-end loaders and similar equipment can support scaffold platforms only when they have been specifically designed by the manufacturer for such use. **1926.451(c)(2)(iv)**

What materials can be used to increase the working level height of employees on supported scaffolds?

Stilts may be used on a large area scaffold. When a guardrail system is used, the guardrail height must be increased in height equal to the height of the stilts. The manufacturer must approve any alterations to the stilts. **1926.452(v)**

Note: A large area scaffold consists of a pole, tube and coupler systems, or a fabricated frame scaffold erected over substantially the entire work area. **1926.451(b)**

Criteria for Suspended Scaffolds

What are suspension scaffolds?

A suspension scaffold contains one or more platforms suspended by ropes or other non-rigid means from an overhead structure, **1926.450(b)**, such as the following scaffolds: single-point, multi-point, multi-level, two-point, adjustable, boatswains' chair, catenary, chimney hoist, continuous run, elevator false car, go-devils, interior hung, masons', and stone setters'.

Are there requirements for suspension scaffolds?

Some of the requirements for all types of suspension scaffolds include:

- Employers must ensure that all employees are trained to recognize the hazards associated with the type of scaffold being used. **1926.451(d)(1)**

- All support devices must rest on surfaces capable of supporting at least four times the load imposed on them by the scaffold when operating at the rated load of the hoist, or at least one-and-a-half times the load imposed on them by the scaffold at the stall capacity of the hoist, whichever is greater. **1926.451(d)(1)**

- A competent person must evaluate all direct connections prior to use to confirm that the supporting surfaces are able to support the imposed load, **1926.451(d)(1)**

- All suspension scaffolds must be tied or otherwise secured to prevent them from swaying, as determined by a competent person. **1926.451(d)**

- Guardrails, a personal fall arrest system, or both must protect each employee more than 10 feet (3.1 meters) above a lower level from falling. **1926.451(g)**

- A competent person must inspect ropes for defects prior to each workshift and after every occurrence that could affect a rope's integrity. **1926.451(d)(10)**

- When scaffold platforms are more than 24 inches (61 centimeters) above or below a point of access, ladders, ramps, walkways, or similar surfaces must be used. **1926.451(e)(1)**

- When using direct access, the surface must not be more than 24 inches (61 centimeters) above or 14 inches (36 cm) horizontally from the surface. **1926.451(e)(8)**

- When lanyards are connected to horizontal lifelines or structural members on single-point or two-point adjustable scaffolds, the scaffold must have additional independent support lines equal in number and strength to the suspension lines and have automatic locking devices. **1926.451(g)(3)(iii)**

- Emergency escape and rescue devices must not be used as working platforms, unless designed to function as suspension scaffolds and emergency systems. **1926.451(d)(19)**

Are there specific requirements for counterweights?

Counterweights used to balance adjustable suspension scaffolds must be able to resist at least four times the tipping moment imposed by the scaffold operating at either the rated load of the hoist, or one-and-a-half (minimum) times the tipping moment imposed by the scaffold operating at the stall load of the hoist, whichever is greater. **1926.451(a)(2)**

Only those items specifically designed as counterweights must be used. **1926.451(d)(3)(iii)**

Counterweights used for suspended scaffolds must be made of materials that can not be easily dislocated. Flowable material, such as sand or water, cannot be used. **1926.451(d)(3)(ii)**

Counterweights must be secured by mechanical means to the outrigger beams. **1926.451(d)(3)(iv)**

Vertical lifelines must not be fastened to counterweights. **1926.451(g)(3)(i)**

Can sand, masonry units, or rolls of roofing felt be used for counterweights?

No. Such materials cannot be used as counterweights. **1926.451(d)(3)(ii) and (iii)**

What are the specific requirements for outrigger beams?

Outrigger beams (thrustouts) are the structural members of a suspension or outrigger scaffold that provide support. **1926.450(b)** They must be placed perpendicular to their bearing support. **1926.451(d)(3)(viii)**

Where do tiebacks for outrigger beams, cornice hooks, roof hooks, roof irons, parapet clamps, or similar devices need to be secured?

Tiebacks must be secured to a structurally sound anchorage on the building or structure. Sound anchorages do **not** include standpipes, vents, other piping systems, or electrical conduit. **1926.451(d)(3)(ix) and (d)(5)**

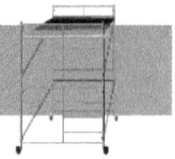

How do tiebacks need to be installed?

A single tieback must be installed perpendicular to the face of the building or structure. Two tiebacks installed at opposing angles are required when a perpendicular tieback cannot be installed. **1926.451(d)(3)(x)**

What are the requirements for suspension ropes?

The suspension ropes must be long enough to allow the scaffold to be lowered to the level below without the rope passing through the hoist, or the end of the rope configured to prevent the end from passing through the hoist. **1926.451(d)(6)**

The standard prohibits using repaired wire. **1926.451(d)(7)**

Drum hoists must contain no less than four wraps of the rope at the lowest point. **1926.451(d)(6)**

Employers must replace wire rope when the following conditions exist: kinks; six randomly broken wires in one rope lay or three broken wires in one strand in one lay; one third of the original diameter of the outside wires is lost; heat damage; evidence that the secondary brake has engaged the rope; and any other physical damage that impairs the function and strength of the rope. **1926.451(d)(10)**

Suspension ropes supporting adjustable suspension scaffolds must be a diameter large enough to provide sufficient surface area for the functioning of brake and hoist mechanisms. **1926.451(f)(10)**

Suspension ropes must be shielded from heat-producing processes. **1926.451(f)(11)**

What are some of the requirements for power-operated suspension scaffold hoists?

Power-operated hoists used to raise or lower a suspended scaffold must be tested and listed by a qualified testing laboratory. **1926.451(d)(13)**

The stall load of any scaffold hoist must not exceed three times its rated load. **1926.451(a)(5)** The stall load is the load at which the prime-mover (motor or engine) of a power-operated hoist stalls or the power to the prime-mover is automatically disconnected. **1926.451(b)**

Gasoline power-operated hoists or equipment are not permitted. **1926.451(d)(14)**

Drum hoists must contain no less than four wraps of suspension rope at the lowest point of scaffold travel. **1926.451(d)(6)**

Gears and brakes must be enclosed. **1926.451(d)(15)**

An automatic braking and locking device, in addition to the operating brake, must engage when a hoist makes an instantaneous change in momentum or an accelerated overspeed. **1926.451(d)(16)**

What are some of the requirements for manually operated suspension scaffold hoists?

Manually operated hoists used to raise or lower a suspended scaffold must be tested and listed by a qualified testing laboratory. **1926.451(d)(13)**

These hoists require a positive crank force to descend. **1926.451(d)(17)**

When can welding be done from a suspension scaffold?

Welding can be done from suspended scaffolds when

- A grounding conductor is connected from the scaffold to the structure and is at least the size of the welding lead;
- The grounding conductor is not attached in series with the welding process or the work piece;
- An insulating material covers the suspension wire rope and extends at least four feet (1.2 meters) above the hoist;
- Insulated protective covers cover the hoist;
- The tail line is guided, retained, or both, so that it does not become grounded;
- Each suspension rope is attached to an insulated thimble; and
- Each suspension rope and any other independent lines are insulated from grounding. **1926.451(f)(17)**

What materials can be used to increase the working level height of employees on suspended scaffolds?

No materials or devices may be used to increase the working height on a suspension scaffold. This includes ladders, boxes, and barrels. **1926.451(f)(14) and (15)**

Access Requirements

What are the requirements for access to scaffolds?

Employers must provide access when the scaffold platforms are more than 2 feet (0.6 meters) above or below a point of access. **1926.451(e)(1)**

Direct access is acceptable when the scaffold is not more than 14 inches (36 centimeters) horizontally and not more than 24 inches (61centimeters) vertically from the other surfaces. **1926.451(e)(8)**

The standard prohibits the use of crossbraces as a means of access. **1926.451(e)(1)**

What types of access can be used?

Several types of access are permitted:
• Ladders, such as portable, hook-on, attachable, and stairway **1926.451 (e)(2),**
• Stair towers **1926.451(e)(4),**
• Ramps and walkways **1926.451(e)(5),** and
• Integral prefabricated frames **(1926.451(e)(6).**

What are the access requirements for employees erecting and dismantling supported scaffolds?

Employees erecting and dismantling supported scaffolding must have a safe means of access provided when a competent person has determined the feasibility and analyzed the site conditions. **1926.451(e)**

Use Requirements

Does the standard prohibit any types of scaffolds?

Shore and lean-to scaffolds are strictly prohibited. **1926.451(f)(2)**

Also, employees are prohibited from working on scaffolds covered with snow, ice, or other slippery materials, except to remove these substances. **1926.451(f)(8)**

What are the clearance distances between scaffolds and powerlines?

The standard requires specific clearance distances. See page 42 of this publication and **1926.451(f)(6)** for a table listing those distances.

Fall Protection Requirements

What is fall protection?

Fall protection includes guardrail systems and personal fall arrest systems. Guardrail systems are explained below in another question. Personal fall arrest systems include harnesses, components of the harness/belt such as Dee-rings, and snap hooks, lifelines, and anchorage point. **1926.451(g)(3)**

Vertical or horizontal lifelines may be used. **1926.451(g)(3)(ii) through (iv)**

Lifelines must be independent of support lines and suspension ropes and not attached to the same anchorage point as the support or suspension ropes. **1926.451(g)(3)(iii) and (iv)**

When working from an aerial lift, attach the fall arrest system to the boom or basket. **1926.453(b)(2)(v)**

What are the fall protection requirements for all scaffolds?

Employers must provide fall protection for each employee on a scaffold more than 10 feet (3.1 meters) above a lower level. **1926.451(g)(1)**

A competent person must determine the feasibility and safety of providing fall protection for employees erecting or dismantling supported scaffolds. **1926.451(g)(2)**

How will I know what kind of fall protection to provide for a specific-type of scaffold?

The chart on the next page illustrates the type of fall protection required for specific scaffolds.

Type of Scaffold	Fall Protection Required
Aerial lifts	Personal fall arrest system
Boatswains' chair	Personal fall arrest system
Catenary scaffold	Personal fall arrest system
Crawling board (chicken ladder)	Personal fall arrest system, **or** a guardrail system, **or** by a 3/4 inch (1.9 cm) diameter grabline or equivalent handhold securely fastened beside each crawling board
Float scaffold	Personal fall arrest system
Ladder jack scaffold	Personal fall arrest system
Needle beam scaffold	Personal fall arrest system
Self-contained scaffold	**Both** a personal adjustable scaffold arrest system **and** a guardrail system
Single-point and two-point suspension scaffolds	Both a personal fall arrest system **and** a guardrail system
Supported scaffold	Personal fall arrest system **or** guardrail system
All other scaffolds not specified above	Personal fall arrest system **or** guardrail systems that meet the required criteria

When can personal fall arrest systems be used when working on scaffolding and aerial lifts?

Personal fall arrest systems can be used on scaffolding when there are no guardrail systems. **1926.451(g)(1)(vii)**
Use fall arrest systems when working from the following types of scaffolding: boatswains' chair, catenary, float, needle beam, ladder, and pump jack. **1926.451(g)(1)**
Use fall arrest systems also when working from the boom/basket of an aerial lift. **1926.453(b)(2)(v)**

When are both fall arrest and guardrail systems required?

Fall arrest and guardrail systems must be used when working on single- and two-point adjustable suspension scaffolds and self-contained adjustable scaffolds that are supported by ropes. **1926.451(g)(1)**

Falling Object Protection

What protections from overhead falling objects do the standards require?

To protect employees from falling hand tools, debris, and other small objects, install toeboards, screens, guardrail systems, debris nets, catch platforms, canopy structures, or barricades. In addition, employees must wear hard hats. **1926.451(h)(1) & (2) and (3)**

Specific Scaffold Requirements §1926.452

Are there additional requirements for specific types of scaffolds?

The standard addresses other requirements for specific types of scaffolds such as mobile, ladder, and pump jack, fabricated frame, and tube and coupler scaffolds. These are found in **1926.452**, "Additional Requirements Applicable to Specific Types of Scaffolds."

Aerial Lift Requirements §1926.453

What are aerial lifts?

Vehicle-mounted aerial devices used to elevate employees—such as extensible boom platforms, aerial lifts, articulating boom platforms, and vertical towers—are considered "aerial lifts." **1926.453(a)(1)**

Do aerial lifts and mobile scaffolds have the same requirements?

The **1926.453** and **1926.454** standards apply to aerial lifts. The **1926.451**, **1926.452**, and **1926.454** standards apply to mobile scaffolds.

What are some of the specific requirements for aerial lifts?

Some specific requirements include the following:
- Only authorized personnel can operate aerial lifts.
- The manufacturer or equivalent must certify any modification.
- The insulated portion must not be altered to reduce its insulating value.
- Lift controls must be tested daily.
- Controls must be clearly marked.
- Brakes must be set and outriggers used.
- Boom and basket load limits must not be exceeded.
- Employees must wear personal fall arrest systems, with the lanyard attached to the boom or basket.
- No devices to raise the employee above the basket floor can be used. **1926.453(b)**

What are the training standards for employees who work on scaffolds?

All employees who work on a scaffold must be trained by a person qualified to recognize the hazards associated with the type of scaffold used and to understand the procedures to control and minimize those hazards. **1926.454(a)**

What are the training standards for employees who work, erect, dismantle, move, operate, repair, maintain, or inspect scaffolds?

A competent person must train all employees who erect, disassemble, move, operate, repair, maintain, or inspect scaffolds. Training must cover the nature of the hazards, the correct procedures for erecting, disassembling, moving, operating, repairing, inspecting, and maintaining the type of scaffold in use. **1926.454(b)**

Other recommended training topics include erection and dismantling, planning, personal protective equipment, access, guys and braces, and parts inspection. **Appendix D**

What are the retraining requirements for employees working on scaffolds?

The standard requires retraining when (1) no employee training has taken place for the worksite changes, scaffold changes, or falling object protection changes; or (2) where the employer believes the employee lacks the necessary skill, understanding, or proficiency to work safely. **1926.454(c)**

Why are the Appendices to the Subpart L scaffolding standards important? Do they address standard requirements?

All of the appendices are non-mandatory and contain selection criteria for planks; American National Standards Institute (ANSI) standard references for aerial lifts; criteria for determining the feasibility of providing safe access and fall protection, and training for erectors and dismantlers; and drawings of various types of scaffolds and components.

To summarize, **Appendix A** of **Subpart L** addresses scaffold specifications and provides non-mandatory guidelines to assist employers in complying with Subpart L requirements. These guidelines and tables provide a starting point for designing scaffold systems; however, they do not provide all the information necessary to build a complete system. Therefore, the employer is still responsible for designing and assembling these components so that the completed system meets the final rule requirements in **1926.451(a)**.

Appendix C lists national consensus standards related to aerial, vehicle mounted, manually propelled, self-propelled, mast climbing, and other such devices.

Appendix D serves as a guide to assist employers when evaluating the training needs for employees erecting or dismantling supported scaffolds.

Appendix E provides drawings of particular types of scaffolds and scaffold components as well as graphic illustrations of bracing patterns and tie-spacing patterns.

How can OSHA help me?

OSHA can provide extensive help through a variety of programs, including assistance about safety and health programs, state plans, workplace consultations, voluntary protection programs, strategic partnerships, training and education, and more.

How does safety and health program management help employers and employees?

Effective management of worker safety and health protection is a decisive factor in reducing the extent and severity of work-related injuries and illnesses and their related costs. In fact, an effective safety and health management system forms the basis of good worker protection and can save time and money—about $4 for every dollar spent—and increase productivity.

To assist employers and employees in developing effective safety and health programs, OSHA published recommended Safety and Health Program Management Guidelines (*Federal Register* 54(18):3904-3916, January 26, 1989). These voluntary guidelines can be applied to all worksites covered by OSHA.

The guidelines identify four general elements that are critical to the development of a successful safety and health management program:
- Management leadership and employee participation,
- Worksite analysis,
- Hazard prevention and control, and
- Safety and health training.

The guidelines recommend specific actions under each of these general elements to achieve an effective safety and health program. The *Federal Register* notice is available online at www.osha.gov.

What are state plans?

State plans are OSHA-approved job safety and health programs operated by individual states or territories instead of Federal OSHA. *The Occupational Safety and Health Act of 1970 (OSH Act)* encourages states to develop and operate their own job safety and health plans and permits state enforcement of OSHA standards if the state has an approved plan. Once OSHA approves a state plan, it funds 50 percent of the program's operating costs. State plans must provide standards and enforcement programs, as well as voluntary compliance activities, that are at least as effective as those of Federal OSHA.

There are 26 state plans: 23 cover both private and public (state and local government) employment, and 3 (Connecticut, New Jersey, and New York) cover only the public sector. For more information on state plans, see the listing at the end of this publication, or visit OSHA's website at www.osha.gov.

How can consultation assistance help employers?

In addition to helping employers identify and correct specific hazards, OSHA's consultation service provides free, onsite assistance in developing and implementing effective workplace safety and health management systems that emphasize the

Comprehensive consultation assistance provided by OSHA includes a hazard survey of the worksite and an appraisal of all aspects of the employer's existing safety and health management system. In addition, the service offers assistance to employers in developing and implementing an effective safety and health management system. Employers also may receive training and education services, as well as limited assistance away from the worksite.

Who can get consultation assistance and what does it cost?

Consultation assistance is available to small employers (with fewer than 250 employees at a fixed site and no more than 500 corporatewide) who want help in establishing and maintaining a safe and healthful workplace.

Funded largely by OSHA, the service is provided at no cost to the employer. Primarily developed for smaller employers with more hazardous operations, the consultation service is delivered by state governments employing professional safety and health consultants. No penalties are proposed or citations issued for hazards identified by the consultant. The employer's only obligation is to correct all identified serious hazards within the agreed upon correction time frame. OSHA provides consultation assistance to the employer with the

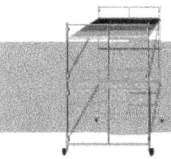

assurance that his or her name and firm and any information about the workplace will not be routinely reported to OSHA enforcement staff.

Can OSHA assure privacy to an employer who asks for consultation assistance?

OSHA provides consultation assistance to the employer with the assurance that his or her name and firm and any information about the workplace will not be routinely reported to OSHA enforcement staff.

Can an employer be cited for violations after receiving consultation assistance?

If an employer fails to eliminate or control a serious hazard within the agreed-upon time frame, the consultation project manager must refer the situation to the OSHA enforcement office for appropriate action. This is a rare occurrence, however, since employers request the service for the expressed purpose of identifying and fixing hazards in their workplaces.

Does OSHA provide any incentives for seeking consultation assistance?

Yes. Under the consultation program, certain exemplary employers may request participation in OSHA's Safety and Health Achievement Recognition Program (SHARP). Eligibility for participation in SHARP includes, but is not limited to, receiving a full-service, comprehensive consultation visit, correcting all identified hazards, and developing an effective safety and health management system.

Employers accepted into SHARP may receive an exemption from programmed inspections (not complaint or accident investigation inspections) for a period of 1 year initially, or 2 years upon renewal. For more information concerning consultation assistance, see the list of consultation directory at the end of this publication, contact your regional or area OSHA office, or visit OSHA's website at www.osha.gov.

What are the Voluntary Protection Programs?

Voluntary Protection Programs (VPPs) represent one part of OSHA's effort to extend worker protection beyond the minimum required by OSHA standards. VPP—along with onsite consultation services, full-service area offices, and OSHA's Strategic Partnership Program (OSPP)—represents a cooperative approach which, when coupled with an effective enforcement program, expands worker protection to help meet the goals of the *OSH Act.*

How do the Voluntary Protection Programs work?

There are three levels of VPPs: Star, Merit, and Demonstration. All are designed to do the following:
- Recognize employers who have successfully developed and implemented effective and comprehensive safety and health management systems;
- Encourage these employers to continuously improve their safety and health management systems;
- Motivate other employers to achieve excellent safety and health results in the same outstanding way; and
- Establish a relationship between employers, employees, and OSHA that is based on cooperation.

How does VPP help employers and employees?

VPP participation can mean the following:
- Reduced numbers of worker fatalities, injuries, and illnesses;
- Lost-workday case rates generally 50 percent below industry averages;
- Lower workers' compensation and other injury- and illness-related costs;
- Improved employee motivation to work safely, leading to a better quality of life at work;
- Positive community recognition and interaction;
- Further improvement and revitalization of already good safety and health programs; and a
- Positive relationship with OSHA.

How does OSHA monitor VPP sites?

OSHA reviews an employer's VPP application and conducts a VPP Onsite Evaluation to verify that the safety and health management systems described are operating effectively at the site. OSHA conducts onsite evaluations on a regular basis, annually for participants at the Demonstration level, every 18 months for Merit, and every 3 to 5 years for Star. Each February, all participants must send a copy of their most recent annual evaluation to their OSHA regional office. This evaluation must include the worksite's record of injuries and illnesses for the past year.

Can OSHA inspect an employer who is participating in the VPP?

Sites participating in VPP are not scheduled for regular, programmed inspections. OSHA handles any employee complaints, serious accidents, or significant chemical releases that may occur at VPP sites according to routine enforcement procedures.

Additional information on VPP is available from OSHA national, regional, and area offices, listed at the end of this booklet. Also, see Outreach on OSHA's website at www.osha.gov.

How can a partnership with OSHA improve worker safety and health?

OSHA has learned firsthand that voluntary, cooperative partnerships with employers, employees, and unions can be a useful alternative to traditional enforcement and an effective way to reduce worker deaths, injuries, and illnesses. This is especially true when a partnership leads to the development and implementation of comprehensive workplace safety and health management system.

What is OSHA's Strategic Partnership Program (OSPP)?

OSHA Strategic Partnerships are alliances among labor, management, and government to foster improvements in workplace safety and health. These partnerships are voluntary, cooperative relationships between OSHA, employers, employee representatives, and others such as trade unions, trade and professional associations, universities, and other government agencies. OSPPs are the newest member of OSHA's family of cooperative programs.

What do OSPPs do?

These partnerships encourage, assist, and recognize the efforts of the partners to eliminate serious workplace hazards and achieve a high level of worker safety and health. Whereas OSHA's Consultation Program and VPP entail one-on-one relationships between OSHA and individual worksites, most strategic partnerships seek to have a broader impact by building cooperative relationships with groups of employers and employees.

Are there different kinds of OSPPs?

There are two major types:
• Comprehensive, which focus on establishing comprehensive safety and health management systems at partnering worksites; and
• Limited, which help identify and eliminate hazards associated with worker deaths, injuries, and illnesses, or have goals other than establishing comprehensive worksite safety and health programs.

OSHA is interested in creating new OSPPs at the national, regional, and local levels. OSHA also has found limited partnerships to be valuable. Limited partnerships might address the elimination or control of a specific industry hazard.

What are the benefits of participation in the OSHA Strategic Partnership Program?

Like VPP, OSPP can mean the following:
• Fewer worker fatalities, injuries, and illnesses;
• Lower workers' compensation and other injury- and illness-related costs;
• Improved employee motivation to work safely, leading to a better quality of life at work and enhanced productivity;
• Positive community recognition and interaction;
• Development of or improvement in safety and health management systems; and
• Positive interaction with OSHA.

For more information about this program, contact your nearest OSHA office or go to the agency website at www.osha.gov.

Does OSHA have occupational safety and health training for employers and employees?

Yes. The OSHA Training Institute in Des Plaines, IL, provides basic and advanced training and education in safety and health for federal and state compliance officers, state consultants, other federal agency personnel, and private-sector employers, employees, and their representatives.

Institute courses cover diverse safety and health topics including electrical hazards, machine guarding, personal protective equipment, ventilation, and ergonomics. The facility includes classrooms, laboratories, a library, and an audiovisual unit. The laboratories contain various demonstrations and equipment, such as power presses, woodworking and welding shops, a complete industrial ventilation unit, and a sound demonstration laboratory. More than 57 courses dealing with subjects such as safety and health in the construction industry and methods of compliance with OSHA standards are available for personnel in the private sector.

In addition, OSHA's 73 area offices are full-service centers offering a variety of informational services such as personnel for speaking engagements, publications, audiovisual aids on workplace hazards, and technical advice.

For more information on grants, training, and education, write: OSHA Training Institute, Office of Training and Education, 1555 Times Drive, Des Plaines, IL 60018; call (847) 297-4810; or see **Outreach** on OSHA's website at www.osha.gov.

Does OSHA give money to organizations for training and education?

OSHA awards grants through its Susan Harwood Training Grant Program to nonprofit organizations to provide safety and health training and education to employers and workers in the workplace. The grants focus on programs that will educate workers and employers in small business (fewer than 250 employees), training workers and employers about new OSHA standards or about high risk activities or hazards. Grants are awarded for 1 year and may be renewed for an additional 12 months depending on whether the grantee has performed satisfactorily.

OSHA expects each organization awarded a grant to develop a training and/or education program that addresses a safety and health topic named by OSHA, recruit workers and employers for the training, and conduct the training. Grantees are also expected to follow up with people who have been trained to find out what changes were made to reduce the hazards in their workplaces as a result of the training.

Each year OSHA has a national competition that is announced in the *Federal Register* and on the Internet at www.osha-slc.gov/Training/sharwood/sharwood.html. If you do not have access to the Internet, you can contact the OSHA Office of Training and Education, 1555 Times Drive, Des Plaines, Illinois 60018, (847) 297-4810, for more information.

Does OSHA have other assistance materials available?

Yes. OSHA has a variety of materials and tools available on its website at www.osha.gov. These include e-Tools, Expert Advisors, Electronic Compliance Assistance Tools (e-CATs), Technical Links, regulations, directives, publications, videos, and other information for employers and employees. OSHA's software programs and compliance assistance tools walk you through challenging safety and health issues and common problems to find the best solutions for your workplace. OSHA's comprehensive publications program includes more than 100 titles to help you understand OSHA requirements and programs.

OSHA's CD-ROM includes standards, interpretations, directives, and more and can be purchased on CD-ROM from the U.S. Government Printing Office. To order, write to the Superintendent of Documents, U.S. Government Printing Office, Washington, DC 20402, or phone (202) 512-1800. Specify OSHA Regulations, Documents and Technical Information on CD-ROM (ORDT), GPO Order No. S/N 729-013-00000-5.

What do I do in case of an emergency? Or if I need to file a complaint?

To report an emergency, file a complaint, or seek OSHA advice, assistance, or products, call (800) 321-OSHA or contact your nearest OSHA regional or area office listed at the end of this publication. The teletypewriter (TTY) number is (877) 889-5627.

You can also file a complaint online and obtain more information on OSHA federal and state programs by visiting OSHA's website at www.osha.gov.

REGION I
(CT,* ME, MA, NH, RI, VT*)
JFK Federal Building, Room E340
Boston, MA 02203
(617) 565-9860

REGION II
(NJ,* PR,* VI*)
201 Varick Street, Room 670
New York, NY 10014
(212) 337-2378

REGION III
(DE, DC, MD,* PA,* VA,* WV)
The Curtis Center
170 S. Independence Mall West
Suite 740 West
Philadelphia, PA 19106-3309
(215) 861-4900

REGION IV
(AL, FL, GA, KY,* MS, NC,* SC,* TN*)
Atlanta Federal Center
61 Forsyth Street, SW, Room 6T50
Atlanta, GA 30303
(404) 562-2300

REGION V
(IL, IN,* MI,* MN,* OH, WI)
230 South Dearborn Street, Room 3244
Chicago, IL 60604
(312) 353-2220

REGION VI
(AR, LA, NM,* OK, TX)
525 Griffin Street, Room 602
Dallas, TX 75202
(214) 767-4731 or 4736 x224

REGION VII
(IA,* KS, MO, NE)
City Center Square
1100 Main Street, Suite 800
Kansas City, MO 64105
(816) 426-5861

REGION VIII
(CO, MT, ND, SD, UT,* WY*)
1999 Broadway, Suite 1690
Denver, CO 80202-5716
(303) 844-1600

REGION IX
(American Samoa, AZ,* CA,* Guram, HI,* NV*)
71 Stevenson Street, Room 420
San Francisco, CA 94105
(415) 975-4310

REGION X
(AK,* ID, OR,* WA*)
1111 Third Avenue, Suite 715
Seattle, WA 98101-3212
(206) 553-5930

Anchorage, AK	(907) 271-5152	Hasbrouck Heights, NJ	(201) 288-1700
Birmingham, AL	(205) 731-1534	Marlton, NJ	(856) 757-5181
Mobile, AL	(251) 441-6131	Parsippany, NJ	(973) 263-1003
Little Rock, AR	(501) 324-6291(5818)	Carson City, NV	(775) 885-6963
Phoenix, AZ	(602) 640-2348	Albany, NY	(518) 464-4338
San Diego, CA	(619) 557-5909	Bayside, NY	(718) 279-9060
Sacramento, CA	(916) 566-7471	Bowmansville, NY	(716) 684-3891
Denver, CO	(303) 844-5285	New York, NY	(212) 337-2636
Greenwood Village, CO	(303) 843-4500	North Syracuse, NY	(315) 451-0808
Bridgeport, CT	(203) 579-5581	Tarrytown, NY	(914) 524-7510
Hartford, CT	(860) 240-3152	Westbury, NY	(516) 334-3344
Wilmington, DE	(302) 573-6518	Cincinnati, OH	(513) 841-4132
Fort Lauderdale, FL	(954) 424-0242	Cleveland, OH	(216) 522-3818
Jacksonville, FL	(904) 232-2895	Columbus, OH	(614) 469-5582
Tampa, FL	(813) 626-1177	Toledo, OH	(419) 259-7542
Savannah, GA	(912) 652-4393	Oklahoma City, OK	(405) 278-9560
Smyrna, GA	(770) 984-8700	Portland, OR	(503) 326-2251
Tucker, GA	(770) 493-6644/	Allentown, PA	(610) 776-0592
	6742/8419	Erie, PA	(814) 833-5758
Des Moines, IA	(515) 284-4794	Harrisburg, PA	(717) 782-3902
Boise, ID	(208) 321-2960	Philadelphia, PA	(215) 597-4955
Calumet City, IL	(708) 891-3800	Pittsburgh, PA	(412) 395-4903
Des Plaines, IL	(847) 803-4800	Wilkes-Barre, PA	(570) 826-6538
Fairview Heights, IL	(618) 632-8612	Guaynabo, PR	(787) 277-1560
North Aurora, IL	(630) 896-8700	Providence, RI	(401) 528-4669
Peoria, IL	(309) 671-7033	Columbia, SC	(803) 765-5904
Indianapolis, IN	(317) 226-7290	Nashville, TN	(615) 781-5423
Wichita, KS	(316) 269-6644	Austin, TX	(512) 916-5783
Frankfort, KY	(502) 227-7024		(5788)
Baton Rouge, LA	(225) 389-0474	Corpus Christi, TX	(361) 888-3420
	(0431)	Dallas, TX	(214) 320-2400
Braintree, MA	(617) 565-6924		(2558)
Methuen, MA	(617) 565-8110	El Paso, TX	(915) 534-6251
Springfield, MA	(413) 785-0123	Fort Worth, TX	(817) 428-2470
Linthicum, MD	(410) 865-2055/2056		(485-7647)
Bangor, ME	(207) 941-8177	Houston, TX	(281) 591-2438
Portland, ME	(207) 780-3178		(2787)
August, ME	(207) 622-8417	Houston, TX	(281) 286-0583/
Lansing, MI	(517) 327-0904		0584 (5922)
Minneapolis, MN	(612) 664- 5460	Lubbock, TX	(806) 472-7681
Kansas City, MO	(816) 483-9531		(7685)
St. Louis, MO	(314) 425-4249	Salt Lake City, UT	(801) 530-6901
Jackson, MS	(601) 965-4606	Norfolk, VA	(757) 441-3820
Billings, MT	(406) 247-7494	Bellevue, WA	(206) 553-7520
Raleigh, NC	(919) 856-4770	Appleton, WI	(920) 734-4521
Omaha, NE	(402) 221-3182	Eau Claire, WI	(715) 832-9019
Bismark, ND	(701) 250-4521	Madison, WI	(608) 264-5388
Concord, NH	(603) 225-1629	Milwaukee, WI	(414) 297-3315
Avenel, NJ	(732) 750-3270	Charleston, WV	(304) 347-5937

Alaska
Alaska Department of Labor
and Workforce Development
Commissioner (907) 465-2700 Fax: (907) 465-2784
Program Director (907) 269-4904
Fax: (907) 269-4915

Arizona
Industrial Commission of Arizona
Director, ICA(602) 542-4411 Fax: (602) 542-1614
Program Director (602) 542-5795
Fax: (602) 542-1614

California
California Department of Industrial Relations
Director (415) 703-5050 Fax:(415) 703-5114
Chief (415) 703-5100 Fax: (415) 703-5114
Manager, Cal/OSHA Program Office
(415) 703-5177 Fax: (415) 703-5114

Connecticut
Connecticut Department of Labor
Commissioner (860) 566-5123 Fax: (860) 566-1520
Conn-OSHA Director (860) 566-4550
Fax: (860) 566-6916

Hawaii
Hawaii Department of Labor
and Industrial Relations
Director (808) 586-8844 Fax: (808) 586-9099
Administrator (808) 586-9116 Fax: (808) 586-9104

Indiana
Indiana Department of Labor
Commissioner (317) 232-2378 Fax: (317) 233-3790
Deputy Commissioner (317) 232-3325
Fax: (317) 233-3790

Iowa
Iowa Division of Labor
Commissioner (515) 281-6432 Fax: (515) 281-4698
Administrator (515) 281-3469 Fax: (515) 281-7995

Kentucky
Kentucky Labor Cabinet
Secretary (502) 564-3070 Fax: (502) 564-5387
Federal-State Coordinator (502) 564-3070 ext.240
Fax: (502) 564-1682

Maryland
Maryland Division of Labor and Industry
Commissioner (410) 767-2999 Fax: (410) 767-2300
Deputy Commissioner (410) 767-2992
Fax: 767-2003
Assistant Commissioner, MOSH (410) 767-2215
Fax: 767-2003

Michigan
Michigan Department of Consumer
and Industry Services
Director (517) 322-1814 Fax: (517)322-1775

Minnesota
Minnesota Department of Labor and Industry
Commissioner (651) 296-2342 Fax: (651) 282-5405
Assistant Commissioner (651) 296-6529
Fax: (651) 282-5293
Administrative Director, OSHA Management Team
(651) 282-5772 Fax: (651) 297-2527

Nevada
Nevada Division of Industrial Relations
Administrator (775) 687-3032 Fax: (775) 687-6305
Chief Administrative Officer (702) 486-9044
Fax:(702) 990-0358
[Las Vegas (702) 687-5240]

New Jersey
New Jersey Department of Labor
Commissioner (609) 292-2975 Fax: (609) 633-9271
Assistant Commissioner (609) 292-2313
Fax: (609) 1314
Program Director, PEOSH (609) 292-3923
Fax: (609) 292-4409

New Mexico
New Mexico Environment Department
Secretary (505) 827-2850 Fax: (505) 827-2836
Chief (505) 827-4230 Fax: (505) 827-4422

New York
New York Department of Labor
Acting Commissioner (518) 457-2741
Fax: (518) 457-6908
Division Director (518) 457-3518
Fax: (518) 457-6908

North Carolina
North Carolina Department of Labor
Commissioner (919) 807-2900 Fax: (919) 807-2855
Deputy Commissioner, OSH Director
(919) 807-2861 Fax: (919) 807-2855
OSH Assistant Director (919) 807-2863
Fax:(919) 807-2856

Oregon
Oregon Occupational Safety and Health Division
Administrator (503) 378-3272 Fax: (503) 947-7461
Deputy Administrator for Policy (503) 378-3272
Fax: (503) 947-7461
Deputy Administrator for Operations (503)
378-3272 Fax: (503) 947-7461

Puerto Rico
Puerto Rico Department of Labor
and Human Resources
Secretary (787) 754-2119 Fax: (787) 753-9550
Assistant Secretary for Occupational Safety
and Health
(787) 756-1100, 1106 / 754-2171
Fax: (787) 767-6051
Deputy Director for Occupational Safety and Health
(787) 756-1100, 1106 / 754-2188
Fax: (787) 767-6051

South Carolina
South Carolina Department of Labor, Licensing,
and Regulation
Director (803) 896-4300 Fax: (803) 896-4393
Program Director (803) 734-9644
Fax: (803) 734-9772

Tennessee
Tennessee Department of Labor
Commissioner (615) 741-2582 Fax: (615) 741-5078
Acting Program Director (615) 741-2793
Fax: (615) 741-3325

Utah
Utah Labor Commission
Commissioner (801) 530-6901 Fax: (801) 530-7906
Administrator (801) 530-6898 Fax: (801) 530-6390

Vermont
Vermont Department of Labor and Industry
Commissioner (802) 828-2288 Fax: (802) 828-2748
Project Manager (802) 828-2765
Fax: (802) 828-2195

Virgin Islands
Virgin Islands Department of Labor
Acting Commissioner (340) 773-1990
Fax: (340) 773-1858
Program Director (340) 772-1315
Fax: (340) 772-4323

Virginia
Virginia Department of Labor and Industry
Commissioner (804) 786-2377 Fax: (804) 371-6524
Director, Office of Legal Support (804) 786-9873
Fax: (804) 786-8418

Washington
Washington Department of Labor and Industries
Director (360) 902-4200 Fax: (360) 902-4202
Assistant Director [PO Box 44600] (360) 902-5495
Fax: (360) 902-5529
Program Manager, Federal-State Operations
[PO Box 44600]
(360) 902-5430 Fax: (360) 902-5529

Wyoming
Wyoming Department of Employment
Safety Administrator (307) 777-7786
Fax: (307) 777-3646

Alabama
(205) 348-3033
(205) 348-3049 FAX

Alaska
(907) 269-4957
(907) 269-4950 FAX

Arizona
(602) 542-1695
(602) 542-1614FAX

Arkansas
(501) 682-4522
(501) 682-4532 FAX

California
(415) 703-5270
(415) 703-4596 FAX

Colorado
(970) 491-6151
(970) 491-7778 FAX

Connecticut
(860) 566-4550
(860) 566-6916 FAX

Delaware
(302) 761-8219
(302) 761-6601 FAX

District of Columbia
(202) 576-6339
(202) 576-7579 FAX

Florida
Phone: 813-974-9962

Georgia
(404) 894-2643
(404) 894-8275 FAX

Guam
011 (671) 475-0136
011 (671) 477-2988 FAX

Hawaii
(808) 586-9100
(808) 586-9099 FAX

Idaho
(208) 426-3283
(208) 426-4411 FAX

Illinois
(312) 814-2337
(312) 814-7238 FAX

Indiana
(317) 232-2688
(317) 232-3790 FAX

Iowa
(515) 281-7629
(515) 281-5522 FAX

Kansas
(785) 296-7476
(785) 296-1775 FAX

Kentucky
(502) 564-6895
(502) 564-6103 FAX

Louisiana
(225) 342-9601
(225) 342-5158 FAX

Maine
(207) 624-6460
(207) 624-6449 FAX

Maryland
(410) 880-4970
(301) 483-8332 FAX

Massachusetts
(617) 727-3982
(617) 727-4581 FAX

Michigan
(517) 322-1809
(517) 322-1374 FAX

Minnesota
(612) 297-2393
(612) 297-1953 FAX

Mississippi
(601) 987-3981
(601) 987-3890 FAX

Missouri
(573) 751-3403
(573) 751-3721 FAX

Montana
(406) 444-6418
(406) 444-4140 FAX

Nebraska
(402) 471-4717
(402) 471-5039 FAX

Nevada
(702) 486-9140
(702) 990-0362 FAX

New Hampshire
(603) 271-2024
(603) 271-2667 FAX

New Jersey
(609) 292-3923
(609) 292-4409 FAX

New Mexico
(505) 827-4230
(505) 827-4422 FAX

New York
(518) 457-2238
(518) 457-3454 FAX

North Carolina
(919) 807-2905
(919) 807-2902 FAX

North Dakota
(701) 328-5188
(701) 328-5200 FAX

Ohio
1-800-282-1425 or 614-644-2631
614-644-3133 FAX

Oklahoma
(405) 528-1500
(405) 528-5751 FAX

Oregon
(503) 378-3272
(503) 378-5729 FAX

Pennsylvania
(724) 357-2396
(724) 357-2385 FAX

Puerto Rico
(787) 754-2171
(787) 767-6051 FAX

Rhode Island
(401) 222-2438
(401) 222-2456 FAX

South Carolina
(803) 734-9614
(803) 734-9741 FAX

South Dakota
(605) 688-4101
(605) 688-6290 FAX

Tennessee
(615) 741-7036
(615) 532-2997 FAX

Texas
(512) 804-4640
(512) 804-4641 FAX
OSHCON Request Line: 800-687-7080

Utah
(801) 530-6901
(801) 530-6992 FAX

Vermont
(802) 828-2765
(802) 828-2195 FAX

Virginia
(804) 786-6359
(804) 786-8418 FAX

Virgin Islands
(340) 772-1315
(340) 772-4323 FAX

Washington
(360) 902-5638
(360) 902-5459 FAX

West Virginia
(304) 558-7890
(304) 558-9711 FAX

Wisconsin (Health)
(608) 266-8579
(608) 266-9383 FAX

Wisconsin (Safety)
(262) 523-3040 1-800-947-0553
(262) 523-3046 FAX

Wyoming
(307) 777-7786
(307) 777-3646 FAX

Index

The following is a guide to the "Safety Standards for Scaffolds Used in the Construction Industry" Standard:

23

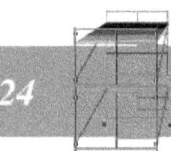

This guideline is to assist the compliance officer
to determine if there is an effective project plan to qualify for a Focused Inspection.

	YES/NO

PROJECT SAFETY AND HEALTH COORDINATION: Are there procedures in place by the general contractor, prime contractor, or other such entity to ensure that all employers provide adequate protection for their employees?

Is there a DESIGNATED COMPETENT PERSON responsible for the implementation and monitoring of the project safety and health plan who is capable of identifying existing and predictable hazards and has authority to take prompt corrective measures?

PROJECT SAFETY AND HEALTH PROGRAM/PLAN* that complies with 1926 Subpart C and addresses, based upon the size and complexity of the project, the following:

_____ Project Safety Analysis at initiation and at critical stages that describes the sequence, procedures, and responsible individuals for safe construction.

_____ Identification of work/activities requiring planning, design, inspection, or supervision by an engineer, competent person, or other professional.

_____ Evaluation monitoring of subcontractors to determine conformance with the Project Plan.(The Project Plan may include, or be utilized by subcontractors.)

_____ Supervisor and employee training according to the Project Plan including recognition, reporting, and avoidance of hazards, and applicable standards.

_____ Procedures for controlling hazardous operations such as: cranes, scaffolding, trenches, confined spaces, hot work, explosives, hazardous materials, leading edges, etc.

_____ Documentation of: training, permits, hazard reports, inspections, uncorrected hazards, incidents, and near misses.

_____ Employee involvement in the hazard: analysis, prevention, avoidance, correction, and reporting.

_____ Project emergency response plan.

* FOR EXAMPLES, SEE OWNER AND CONTRACTOR ASSOCIATION MODEL PROGRAMS, ANSI A10.33, A10.38, ETC.

The walkaround and interviews confirmed that the Plan has been implemented, including:

_____ The four leading hazards are addressed: falls, struck by, caught in\between, electrical.

_____ Hazards are identified and corrected with preventative measures instituted in a timely manner.

_____ Employees and supervisors are knowledgeable of the project safety and health plan, avoidance of hazards, applicable standards, and their rights and responsibilities.

THE PROJECT QUALIFIED FOR A FOCUSED INSPECTION.

PART 1926—[AMENDED]

1. Subpart L of Part 1926 is revised to read as follows:

SUBPART L—SCAFFOLDS

Sec.

Authority: Section 107, *Contract Work Hours and Safety Standards Act* (Construction Safety Act) (40 U.S.C. 333); Secs. 4, 6, 8, *Occupational Safety and Health Act of 1970* (29 U.S.C. 653, 655, 657); Secretary of Labor's Order No. 1-90 (55 FR 9033);and 29 CFR Part 1911.

SUBPART L—SCAFFOLDS

§1926.450 Scope, application and definitions applicable to this Subpart.

(a) **Scope and application.** This subpart applies to all scaffolds used in workplaces covered by this Part. It does not apply to crane or derrick suspended personnel platforms, which are covered by §1926.550(g). The criteria for aerial lifts are set out exclusively in §1926.453.

(b) **Definitions.** "Adjustable suspension scaffold" means a suspension scaffold equipped with a hoist(s) that can be operated by an employee(s) on the scaffold.

"Bearer (putlog)" means a horizontal transverse scaffold member (which may be supported by ledgers or runners) upon which the scaffold platform rests and which joins scaffold uprights, posts, poles, and similar members.

"Boatswains' chair" means a single-point adjustable suspension scaffold consisting of a seat or sling designed to support one employee in a sitting position.

"Body belt (safety belt)" means a strap with means both for securing it about the waist and for attaching it to a lanyard, lifeline, or deceleration device.

"Body harness" means a design of straps which may be secured about the employee in a manner to distribute the fall arrest forces over at least the thighs, pelvis, waist, chest and shoulders, with means for attaching it to other components of a personal fall arrest system.

"Brace" means a rigid connection that holds one scaffold member in a fixed position with respect to another member, or to a building or structure.

"Bricklayers' square scaffold" means a supported scaffold composed of framed squares which support a platform.

"Carpenters' bracket scaffold" means a supported scaffold consisting of a platform supported by brackets attached to building or structural walls.

"Catenary scaffold" means a suspension scaffold consisting of a platform supported by two essentially horizontal and parallel ropes attached to structural members of a building or other structure. Additional support may be provided by vertical pickups.

"Chimney hoist" means a multi-point adjustable suspension scaffold used to provide access to work inside chimneys. (See "Multi-point adjustable suspension scaffold".)

"Cleat" means a structural block used at the end of a platform to prevent the platform from slipping off its supports. Cleats are also used to provide footing on sloped surfaces such as crawling boards.

"Competent person" means one who is capable of identifying existing and predictable hazards in the surroundings or working conditions which are unsanitary, hazardous, or dangerous to employees, and who has authorization to take prompt corrective measures to eliminate them.

"Continuous run scaffold" (Run scaffold) means a two-point or multi-point adjustable suspension scaffold constructed using a series of interconnected braced scaffold members or supporting structures erected to form a continuous scaffold.

"Coupler" means a device for locking together the tubes of a tube and coupler scaffold.

"Crawling board (chicken ladder)" means a supported scaffold consisting of a plank with cleats spaced and secured to provide footing, for use on sloped surfaces such as roofs.

"Deceleration device" means any mechanism, such as a rope grab, rip-stitch lanyard, specially-woven lanyard, tearing or deforming lanyard, or automatic self-retracting lifeline lanyard, which dissipates a substantial amount of energy during a

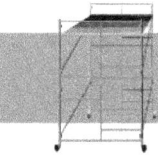

fall arrest or limits the energy imposed on an employee during fall arrest.

"Double pole (independent pole) scaffold" means a supported scaffold consisting of a platform(s) resting on cross beams (bearers) supported by ledgers and a double row of uprights independent of support (except ties, guys, braces) from any structure.

"Equivalent" means alternative designs, materials or methods to protect against a hazard which the employer can demonstrate will provide an equal or greater degree of safety for employees than the methods, materials or designs specified in the standard.

"Eye" or "Eye Splice" means a loop with or without a thimble at the end of a wire rope.

"Exposed power lines" means electrical power lines which are accessible to employees and which are not shielded from contact. Such lines do not include extension cords or power tool cords.

"Fabricated decking and planking" means manufactured platforms made of wood (including laminated wood, and solid sawn wood planks), metal or other materials.

"Fabricated frame scaffold (tubular welded frame scaffold)" means a scaffold consisting of a platform(s) supported on fabricated end frames with integral posts, horizontal bearers, and intermediate members.

"Failure" means load refusal, breakage, or separation of component parts. Load refusal is the point where the ultimate strength is exceeded.

"Float (ship) scaffold" means a suspension scaffold consisting of a braced platform resting on two parallel bearers and hung from overhead supports by ropes of fixed length.

"Form scaffold" means a supported scaffold consisting of a platform supported by brackets attached to formwork.

"Guardrail system" means a vertical barrier, consisting of, but not limited to, toprails, midrails, and posts, erected to prevent employees from falling off a scaffold platform or walkway to lower levels.

"Hoist" means a manual or power-operated mechanical device to raise or lower a suspended scaffold.

"Horse scaffold" means a supported scaffold consisting of a platform supported by construction horses (saw horses). Horse scaffolds constructed of metal are sometimes known as trestle scaffolds.

"Independent pole scaffold" (see "Double pole scaffold").

"Interior hung scaffold" means a suspension scaffold consisting of a platform suspended from the ceiling or roof structure by fixed length supports.

"Ladder jack scaffold" means a supported scaffold consisting of a platform resting on brackets attached to ladders.

"Ladder stand" means a mobile, fixed-size, self-supporting ladder consisting of a wide flat tread ladder in the form of stairs.

"Landing" means a platform at the end of a flight of stairs.

"Large area scaffold" means a pole scaffold, tube and coupler scaffold, systems scaffold, or fabricated frame scaffold erected over substantially the entire work area. For example: a scaffold erected over the entire floor area of a room.

"Lean-to scaffold" means a supported scaffold which is kept erect by tilting it toward and resting it against a building or structure.

"Lifeline" means a component consisting of a flexible line that connects to an anchorage at one end to hang vertically (vertical lifeline), or that connects to anchorages at both ends to stretch horizontally (horizontal lifeline), and which serves as a means for connecting other components of a personal fall arrest system to the anchorage.

"Lower levels" means areas below the level where the employee is located and to which an employee can fall. Such areas include, but are not limited to, ground levels, floors, roofs, ramps, runways, excavations, pits, tanks, materials, water, and equipment.

"Masons' adjustable supported scaffold" (see "Self-contained adjustable scaffold").

"Masons' multi-point adjustable suspension scaffold" means a continuous run suspension scaffold designed and used for masonry operations.

"Maximum intended load" means the total load of all persons, equipment, tools, materials, transmitted loads, and other loads reasonably anticipated to be applied to a scaffold or scaffold component at any one time.

"Mobile scaffold" means a powered or unpowered, portable, caster or wheel-mounted supported scaffold.

"Multi-level suspended scaffold" means a two-point or multi-point adjustable suspension scaffold with a series of platforms at various levels resting on common stirrups.

"Multi-point adjustable suspension scaffold" means a suspension scaffold consisting of a platform(s) which is suspended by more than two ropes from overhead supports and equipped with means to raise and lower the platform to desired work levels. Such scaffolds include chimney hoists.

"Needle beam scaffold" means a platform suspended from needle beams.

"Open sides and ends" means the edges of a platform that are more than 14 inches (36 cm) away horizontally from a sturdy, continuous, vertical surface (such as a building wall) or a sturdy, continuous horizontal surface (such as a floor), or a point of access. Exception: For plastering and lathing operations the horizontal threshold distance is 18 inches (46 cm).

"Outrigger" means the structural member of a supported scaffold used to increase the base width of a scaffold in order to provide support for and increased stability of the scaffold.

"Outrigger beam (Thrustout)" means the structural member of a suspension scaffold or outrigger scaffold which provides support for the scaffold by extending the scaffold point of attachment to a point out and away from the structure or building.

"Outrigger scaffold" means a supported scaffold consisting of a platform resting on outrigger beams (thrustouts) projecting beyond the wall or face of the building or structure, the inboard ends of which are secured inside the building or structure.

"Overhand bricklaying" means the process of laying bricks and masonry units such that the surface of the wall to be jointed is on the opposite side of the wall from the mason, requiring the mason to lean over the wall to complete the work. It includes mason tending and electrical installation incorporated into the brick wall during the overhand bricklaying process.

"Personal fall arrest system" means a system used to arrest an employee's fall. It consists of an anchorage, connectors, a body belt or body harness and may include a lanyard, deceleration device, lifeline, or combinations of these.

"Platform" means a work surface elevated above lower levels. Platforms can be constructed using individual wood planks, fabricated planks, fabricated decks, and fabricated platforms.

"Pole scaffold" (see definitions for "Single-pole

scaffold" and "Double (independent) pole scaffold").

"Power operated hoist" means a hoist which is powered by other than human energy.

"Pump jack scaffold" means a supported scaffold consisting of a platform supported by vertical poles and movable support brackets.

"Qualified" means one who, by possession of a recognized degree, certificate, or professional standing, or who by extensive knowledge, training, and experience, has successfully demonstrated his/her ability to solve or resolve problems related to the subject matter, the work, or the project.

"Rated load" means the manufacturer's specified maximum load to be lifted by a hoist or to be applied to a scaffold or scaffold component.

"Repair bracket scaffold" means a supported scaffold consisting of a platform supported by brackets which are secured in place around the circumference or perimeter of a chimney, stack, tank or other supporting structure by one or more wire ropes placed around the supporting structure.

"Roof bracket scaffold" means a rooftop supported scaffold consisting of a platform resting on angular-shaped supports.

"Runner" (ledger or ribbon)" means the lengthwise horizontal spacing or bracing member which may support the bearers.

"Scaffold" means any temporary elevated platform (supported or suspended) and its supporting structure (including points of anchorage), used for supporting employees or materials or both.

"Self-contained adjustable scaffold" means a combination supported and suspension scaffold consisting of an adjustable platform(s) mounted on an independent supporting frame(s) not a part of the object being worked on, and which is equipped with a means to permit the raising and lowering of the platform(s). Such systems include rolling roof rigs, rolling outrigger systems, and some masons' adjustable supported scaffolds.

"Shore scaffold" means a supported scaffold which is placed against a building or structure and held in place with props.

"Single-point adjustable suspension scaffold" means a suspension scaffold consisting of a platform suspended by one rope from an overhead support and equipped with means to permit the movement of the platform to desired work levels.

"Single-pole scaffold" means a supported scaffold consisting of a platform(s) resting on bearers,

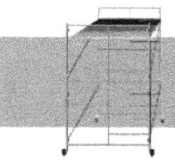

the outside ends of which are supported on runners secured to a single row of posts or uprights, and the inner ends of which are supported on or in a structure or building wall.

"Stair tower (Scaffold stairway/tower)" means a tower comprised of scaffold components and which contains internal stairway units and rest platforms. These towers are used to provide access to scaffold platforms and other elevated points such as floors and roofs.

"Stall load" means the load at which the prime-mover of a power-operated hoist stalls or the power to the prime-mover is automatically disconnected.

"Step, platform, and trestle ladder scaffold" means a platform resting directly on the rungs of step ladders or trestle ladders.

"Stilts" means a pair of poles or similar supports with raised footrests, used to permit walking above the ground or working surface.

"Stonesetters' multi-point adjustable suspension scaffold" means a continuous run suspension scaffold designed and used for stonesetters' operations.

"Supported scaffold" means one or more platforms supported by outrigger beams, brackets, poles, legs, uprights, posts, frames, or similar rigid support.

"Suspension scaffold" means one or more platforms suspended by ropes or other non-rigid means from an overhead structure(s).

"System scaffold" means a scaffold consisting of posts with fixed connection points that accept runners, bearers, and diagonals that can be interconnected at predetermined levels.

"Tank builders' scaffold" means a supported scaffold consisting of a platform resting on brackets that are either directly attached to a cylindrical tank or attached to devices that are attached to such a tank.

"Top plate bracket scaffold" means a scaffold supported by brackets that hook over or are attached to the top of a wall. This type of scaffold is similar to carpenters' bracket scaffolds and form scaffolds and is used in residential construction for setting trusses.

"Tube and coupler scaffold" means a supported or suspended scaffold consisting of a platform(s) supported by tubing, erected with coupling devices connecting uprights, braces, bearers, and runners.

"Tubular welded frame scaffold" (see "Fabricated frame scaffold").

"Two-point suspension scaffold (swing stage)" means a suspension scaffold consisting of a platform supported by hangers (stirrups) suspended by two ropes from overhead supports and equipped with means to permit the raising and lowering of the platform to desired work levels.

"Unstable objects" means items whose strength, configuration, or lack of stability may allow them to become dislocated and shift and therefore may not properly support the loads imposed on them. Unstable objects do not constitute a safe base support for scaffolds, platforms, or employees. Examples include, but are not limited to, barrels, boxes, loose brick, and concrete blocks.

"Vertical pickup" means a rope used to support the horizontal rope in catenary scaffolds.

"Walkway" means a portion of a scaffold platform used only for access and not as a work level.

"Window jack scaffold" means a platform resting on a bracket or jack which projects through a window opening.

§1926.451 **General requirements.** This section does not apply to aerial lifts, the criteria for which are set out in §1926.453.

(a) **Capacity** (1) Except as provided in paragraphs (a)(2), (a)(3), (a)(4), (a)(5) and (g) of this section, each scaffold and scaffold component shall be capable of supporting, without failure, its own weight and at least 4 times the maximum intended load applied or transmitted to it.

(2) Direct connections to roofs and floors, and counterweights used to balance adjustable suspension scaffolds, shall be capable of resisting at least 4 times the tipping moment imposed by the scaffold operating at the rated load of the hoist, or 1.5 (minimum) times the tipping moment imposed by the scaffold operating at the stall load of the hoist, whichever is greater.

(3) Each suspension rope, including connecting hardware, used on non-adjustable suspension scaffolds shall be capable of supporting, without failure, at least 6 times the maximum intended load applied or transmitted to that rope.

(4) Each suspension rope, including connecting hardware, used on adjustable suspension scaffolds shall be capable of supporting, without failure, at least 6 times the maximum intended load applied or transmitted to that rope with the scaffold operating at either the rated load of the hoist, or 2 (minimum) times the stall load of the hoist, whichever is greater.

(1926.451(a) continued)

(5) The stall load of any scaffold hoist shall not exceed 3 times its rated load.

(6) Scaffolds shall be designed by a qualified person and shall be constructed and loaded in accordance with that design. Non-mandatory Appendix A to this subpart contains examples of criteria that will enable an employer to comply with paragraph (a) of this section.

(b) **Scaffold platform construction.**

(1) Each platform on all working levels of scaffolds shall be fully planked or decked between the front uprights and the guardrail supports as follows:

(i) Each platform unit (e.g., scaffold plank, fabricated plank, fabricated deck, or fabricated platform) shall be installed so that the space between adjacent units and the space between the platform and the uprights is no more than 1 inch (2.5 cm) wide, except where the employer can demonstrate that a wider space is necessary (for example, to fit around uprights when side brackets are used to extend the width of the platform).

(ii) Where the employer makes the demonstration provided for in paragraph (b)(1)(i) of this section, the platform shall be planked or decked as fully as possible and the remaining open space between the platform and the uprights shall not exceed 9 inches (24.1 cm).

Exception to paragraph (b)(1): The requirement to provide full planking or decking does not apply to platforms used solely as walkways or solely by employees performing scaffold erection or dismantling. In these situations, only the planking that the employer establishes is necessary to provide safe working conditions is required.

(2) Except as provided in paragraphs (b)(2)(i) and (b)(2)(ii) of this section, each scaffold platform and walkway shall be at least 18 inches (46 cm) wide.

(i) Each ladder jack scaffold, top plate bracket scaffold, roof bracket scaffold, and pump jack scaffold shall be at least 12 inches (30 cm) wide. There is no minimum width requirement for boatswains' chairs.

(ii) Where scaffolds must be used in areas that the employer can demonstrate are so narrow that platforms and walkways cannot be at least 18 inches (46 cm) wide, such platforms and walkways shall be as wide as feasible, and employees on those platforms and walkways shall be protected from fall hazards by the use of guardrails and/or personal fall arrest systems.

(3) Except as provided in paragraphs (b)(3)(i) and (ii) of this section, the front edge of all platforms shall not be more than 14 inches (36 cm) from the face of the work, unless guardrail systems are erected along the front edge and/or personal fall arrest systems are used in accordance with paragraph (g) of this section to protect employees from falling.

(i) The maximum distance from the face for outrigger scaffolds shall be 3 inches (8 cm);

(ii) The maximum distance from the face for plastering and lathing operations shall be 18 inches (46 cm).

(4) Each end of a platform, unless cleated or otherwise restrained by hooks or equivalent means, shall extend over the centerline of its support at least 6 inches (15 cm).

(5) (i) Each end of a platform 10 feet or less in length shall not extend over its support more than 12 inches (30 cm) unless the platform is designed and installed so that the cantilevered portion of the platform is able to support employees and/or materials without tipping, or has guardrails which block employee access to the cantilevered end.

(ii) Each platform greater than 10 feet in length shall not extend over its support more than 18 inches (46 cm), unless it is designed and installed so that the cantilevered portion of the platform is able to support employees without tipping, or has guardrails which block employee access to the cantilevered end.

(6) On scaffolds where scaffold planks are abutted to create a long platform, each abutted end shall rest on a separate support surface. This provision does not preclude the use of common support members, such as "T" sections, to support abutting planks, or hook on platforms designed to rest on common supports.

(7) On scaffolds where platforms are overlapped to create a long platform, the overlap shall occur only over supports, and shall not be less than 12 inches (30 cm) unless the platforms are nailed together or otherwise restrained to prevent movement.

(8) At all points of a scaffold where the platform changes direction, such as turning a corner, any platform that rests on a bearer at an angle other than a right angle shall be laid first, and platforms which rest at right angles over the same bearer shall be laid second, on top of the first platform.

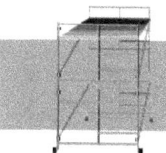

(1926.451(b) continued)

(9) Wood platforms shall not be covered with opaque finishes, except that platform edges may be covered or marked for identification. Platforms may be coated periodically with wood preservatives, fire-retardant finishes, and slip-resistant finishes; however, the coating may not obscure the top or bottom wood surfaces.

(10) Scaffold components manufactured by different manufacturers shall not be intermixed unless the components fit together without force and the scaffold's structural integrity is maintained by the user. Scaffold components manufactured by different manufacturers shall not be modified in order to intermix them unless a competent person determines the resulting scaffold is structurally sound.

(11) Scaffold components made of dissimilar metals shall not be used together unless a competent person has determined that galvanic action will not reduce the strength of any component to a level below that required by paragraph (a)(1) of this section.

(c) **Criteria for supported scaffolds.**

(1) Supported scaffolds with a height to base width (including outrigger supports, if used) ratio of more than four to one (4:1) shall be restrained from tipping by guying, tying, bracing, or equivalent means, as follows:

(i) Guys, ties, and braces shall be installed at locations where horizontal members support both inner and outer legs.

(ii) Guys, ties, and braces shall be installed according to the scaffold manufacturer's recommendations or at the closest horizontal member to the 4:1 height and be repeated vertically at locations of horizontal members every 20 feet (6.1 m) or less thereafter for scaffolds 3 feet (0.91 m) wide or less, and every 26 feet (7.9 m) or less thereafter for scaffolds greater than 3 feet (0.91 m) wide. The top guy, tie or brace of completed scaffolds shall be placed no further than the 4:1 height from the top. Such guys, ties and braces shall be installed at each end of the scaffold and at horizontal intervals not to exceed 30 feet (9.1 m) (measured from one end [not both] towards the other).

(iii) Ties, guys, braces, or outriggers shall be used to prevent the tipping of supported scaffolds in all circumstances where an eccentric load, such as a cantilevered work platform, is applied or is transmitted to the scaffold.

(2) Supported scaffold poles, legs, posts, frames, and uprights shall bear on base plates and mud sills or other adequate firm foundation.

(i) Footings shall be level, sound, rigid, and capable of supporting the loaded scaffold without settling or displacement.

(ii) Unstable objects shall not be used to support scaffolds or platform units.

(iii) Unstable objects shall not be used as working platforms.

(iv) Front-end loaders and similar pieces of equipment shall not be used to support scaffold platforms unless they have been specifically designed by the manufacturer for such use.

(v) Fork-lifts shall not be used to support scaffold platforms unless the entire platform is attached to the fork and the fork-lift is not moved horizontally while the platform is occupied.

(3) Supported scaffold poles, legs, posts, frames, and uprights shall be plumb and braced to prevent swaying and displacement.

(d) **Criteria for suspension scaffolds.**

(1) All suspension scaffold support devices, such as outrigger beams, cornice hooks, parapet clamps, and similar devices, shall rest on surfaces capable of supporting at least 4 times the load imposed on them by the scaffold operating at the rated load of the hoist (or at least 1.5 times the load imposed on them by the scaffold at the stall capacity of the hoist, whichever is greater).

(2) Suspension scaffold outrigger beams, when used, shall be made of structural metal or equivalent strength material, and shall be restrained to prevent movement.

(3) The inboard ends of suspension scaffold outrigger beams shall be stabilized by bolts or other direct connections to the floor or roof deck, or they shall have their inboard ends stabilized by counterweights, except masons' multi-point adjustable suspension scaffold outrigger beams shall not be stabilized by counterweights.

(i) Before the scaffold is used, direct connections shall be evaluated by a competent person who shall confirm, based on the evaluation, that the supporting surfaces are capable of supporting the loads to be imposed. In addition, masons' multi-point adjustable suspension scaffold connections shall be designed by an engineer experienced in such scaffold design.

(ii) Counterweights shall be made of non-flowable material. Sand, gravel and similar materials that can

(1926.451(d) continued)
be easily dislocated shall not be used as counterweights.

(iii) Only those items specifically designed as counterweights shall be used to counterweight scaffold systems. Construction materials such as, but not limited to, masonry units and rolls of roofing felt, shall not be used as counterweights.

(iv) Counterweights shall be secured by mechanical means to the outrigger beams to prevent accidental displacement.

(v) Counterweights shall not be removed from an outrigger beam until the scaffold is disassembled.

(vi) Outrigger beams which are not stabilized by bolts or other direct connections to the floor or roof deck shall be secured by tiebacks.

(vii) Tiebacks shall be equivalent in strength to the suspension ropes.

(viii) Outrigger beams shall be placed perpendicular to its bearing support (usually the face of the building or structure). However, where the employer can demonstrate that it is not possible to place an outrigger beam perpendicular to the face of the building or structure because of obstructions that cannot be moved, the outrigger beam may be placed at some other angle, provided opposing angle tiebacks are used.

(ix) Tiebacks shall be secured to a structurally sound anchorage on the building or structure. Sound anchorages include structural members, but do not include standpipes, vents, other piping systems, or electrical conduit.

(x) Tiebacks shall be installed perpendicular to the face of the building or structure, or opposing angle tiebacks shall be installed. Single tiebacks installed at an angle are prohibited.

(4) Suspension scaffold outrigger beams shall be:

(i) Provided with stop bolts or shackles at both ends;

(ii) Securely fastened together with the flanges turned out when channel iron beams are used in place of I-beams;

(iii) Installed with all bearing supports perpendicular to the beam center line;

(iv) Set and maintained with the web in a vertical position; and

(v) When an outrigger beam is used, the shackle or clevis with which the rope is attached to the outrigger beam shall be placed directly over the center line of the stirrup.

(5) Suspension scaffold support devices such as cornice hooks, roof hooks, roof irons, parapet clamps, or similar devices shall be:

(i) Made of steel, wrought iron, or materials of equivalent strength;

(ii) Supported by bearing blocks; and

(iii) Secured against movement by tiebacks installed at right angles to the face of the building or structure, or opposing angle tiebacks shall be installed and secured to a structurally sound point of anchorage on the building or structure. Sound points of anchorage include structural members, but do not include standpipes, vents, other piping systems, or electrical conduit.

(iv) Tiebacks shall be equivalent in strength to the hoisting rope.

(6) When winding drum hoists are used on a suspension scaffold, they shall contain not less than four wraps of the suspension rope at the lowest point of scaffold travel. When other types of hoists are used, the suspension ropes shall be long enough to allow the scaffold to be lowered to the level below without the rope end passing through the hoist, or the rope end shall be configured or provided with means to prevent the end from passing through the hoist.

(7) The use of repaired wire rope as suspension rope is prohibited.

(8) Wire suspension ropes shall not be joined together except through the use of eye splice thimbles connected with shackles or coverplates and bolts.

(9) The load end of wire suspension ropes shall be equipped with proper size thimbles and secured by eyesplicing or equivalent means.

(10) Ropes shall be inspected for defects by a competent person prior to each workshift and after every occurrence which could affect a rope's integrity. Ropes shall be replaced if any of the following conditions exist:

(i) Any physical damage which impairs the function and strength of the rope.

(ii) Kinks that might impair the tracking or wrapping of rope around the drum(s) or sheave(s).

(iii) Six randomly distributed broken wires in one rope lay or three broken wires in one strand in one rope lay.

(iv) Abrasion, corrosion, scrubbing, flattening or peening causing loss of more than one-third of the original diameter of the outside wires.

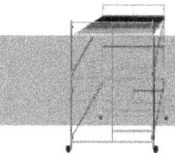

(1926.451(d) continued)

(v) Heat damage caused by a torch or any damage caused by contact with electrical wires.

(vi) Evidence that the secondary brake has been activated during an overspeed condition and has engaged the suspension rope.

(11) Swaged attachments or spliced eyes on wire suspension ropes shall not be used unless they are made by the wire rope manufacturer or a qualified person.

(12) When wire rope clips are used on suspension scaffolds:

(i) There shall be a minimum of 3 wire rope clips installed, with the clips a minimum of 6 rope diameters apart;

(ii) Clips shall be installed according to the manufacturer's recommendations;

(iii) Clips shall be retightened to the manufacturer's recommendations after the initial loading;

(iv) Clips shall be inspected and retightened to the manufacturer's recommendations at the start of each workshift thereafter;

(v) U-bolt clips shall not be used at the point of suspension for any scaffold hoist;

(vi) When U-bolt clips are used, the U-bolt shall be placed over the dead end of the rope, and the saddle shall be placed over the live end of the rope.

(13) Suspension scaffold power-operated hoists and manual hoists shall be tested by a qualified testing laboratory.

(14) Gasoline-powered equipment and hoists shall not be used on suspension scaffolds.

(15) Gears and brakes of power-operated hoists used on suspension scaffolds shall be enclosed.

(16) In addition to the normal operating brake, suspension scaffold power-operated hoists and manually operated hoists shall have a braking device or locking pawl which engages automatically when a hoist makes either of the following uncontrolled movements: an instantaneous change in momentum or an accelerated overspeed.

(17) Manually operated hoists shall require a positive crank force to descend.

(18) Two-point and multi-point suspension scaffolds shall be tied or otherwise secured to prevent them from swaying, as determined to be necessary based on an evaluation by a competent person. Window cleaners' anchors shall not be used for this purpose.

(19) Devices whose sole function is to provide emergency escape and rescue shall not be used as working platforms. (This provision does not preclude the use of systems which are designed to function both as suspension scaffolds and emergency systems.)

(e) **Access.** This paragraph applies to scaffold access for all employees. Access requirements for employees erecting or dismantling supported scaffolds are specifically addressed in paragraph (e)(9) of this section.

(1) When scaffold platforms are more than 2 feet (0.6 m) above or below a point of access, portable ladders, hook-on ladders, attachable ladders, stair towers (scaffold stairways/towers), stairway-type ladders (such as ladder stands), ramps, walkways, integral prefabricated scaffold access, or direct access from another scaffold, structure, personnel hoist, or similar surface shall be used. Crossbraces shall not be used as a means of access.

(2) Portable, hook-on, and attachable ladders (Additional requirements for the proper construction and use of portable ladders are contained in Subpart X of this part—Stairways and Ladders):

(i) Portable, hook-on, and attachable ladders shall be positioned so as not to tip the scaffold;

(ii) Hook-on and attachable ladders shall be positioned so that their bottom rung is not more than 24 inches (61 cm) above the scaffold supporting level;

(iii) When hook-on and attachable ladders are used on a supported scaffold more than 35 feet (10.7 m.) high, they shall have rest platforms at 35-foot (10.7 m) maximum vertical intervals.

(iv) Hook-on and attachable ladders shall be specifically designed for use with the type of scaffold used;

(v) Hook-on and attachable ladders shall have a minimum rung length of 11-1/2 inches (29 cm); and

(vi) Hook-on and attachable ladders shall have uniformly spaced rungs with a maximum spacing between rungs of 16-3/4 inches.

(3) Stairway-type ladders shall:

(i) be positioned such that their bottom step is not more than 24 inches (61 cm) above the scaffold supporting level;

(ii) be provided with rest platforms at 12 foot (3.7 m) maximum vertical intervals;

(iii) have a minimum step width of 16 inches (41 cm), except that mobile scaffold stairway-type ladders shall have a minimum step width of 11 1/2 inches (30 cm); and

(1926.451(e) continued)

(iv) have slip-resistant treads on all steps and landings.

(4) Stairtowers (scaffold stairway/towers) shall be positioned such that their bottom step is not more than 24 inches (61 cm.) above the scaffold supporting level.

(i) A stairrail consisting of a toprail and a midrail shall be provided on each side of each scaffold stairway.

(ii) The toprail of each stairrail system shall also be capable of serving as a handrail, unless a separate handrail is provided.

(iii) Handrails, and toprails that serve as handrails, shall provide an adequate handhold for employees grasping them to avoid falling.

(iv) Stairrail systems and handrails shall be surfaced to prevent injury to employees from punctures or lacerations, and to prevent snagging of clothing.

(v) The ends of stairrail systems and handrails shall be constructed so that they do not constitute a projection hazard.

(vi) Handrails, and toprails that are used as handrails, shall be at least 3 inches (7.6 cm) from other objects.

(vii) Stairrails shall be not less than 28 inches (71 cm) nor more than 37 inches (94 cm) from the upper surface of the stairrail to the surface of the tread, in line with the face of the riser at the forward edge of the tread.

(viii) A landing platform at least 18 inches (45.7 cm) wide by at least 18 inches (45.7 cm) long shall be provided at each level.

(ix) Each scaffold stairway shall be at least 18 inches (45.7 cm) wide between stairrails.

(x) Treads and landings shall have slip-resistant surfaces.

(xi) Stairways shall be installed between 40 degrees and 60 degrees from the horizontal.

(xii) Guardrails meeting the requirements of paragraph (g)(4) of this section shall be provided on the open sides and ends of each landing.

(xiii) Riser height shall be uniform, within 1/4 inch, (0.6 cm) for each flight of stairs. Greater variations in riser height are allowed for the top and bottom steps of the entire system, not for each flight of stairs.

(xiv) Tread depth shall be uniform, within 1/4 inch, for each flight of stairs.

(5) Ramps and walkways.

(i) Ramps and walkways 6 feet (1.8 m) or more above lower levels shall have guardrail systems which comply with Subpart M of this part—Fall Protection;

(ii) No ramp or walkway shall be inclined more than a slope of one (1) vertical to three (3) horizontal (20 degrees above the horizontal).

(iii) If the slope of a ramp or a walkway is steeper than one (1) vertical in eight (8) horizontal, the ramp or walkway shall have cleats not more than fourteen (14) inches (35 cm) apart which are securely fastened to the planks to provide footing.

(6) Integral prefabricated scaffold access frames shall:

(i) Be specifically designed and constructed for use as ladder rungs;

(ii) Have a rung length of at least 8 inches (20 cm);

(iii) Not be used as work platforms when rungs are less than 11-1/2 inches in length, unless each affected employee uses fall protection, or a positioning device, which complies with §1926.502;

(iv) Be uniformly spaced within each frame section;

(v) Be provided with rest platforms at 35-foot (10.7 m) maximum vertical intervals on all supported scaffolds more than 35 feet (10.7 m) high; and

(vi) Have a maximum spacing between rungs of 16 3/4 inches (43 cm). Non-uniform rung spacing caused by joining end frames together is allowed, provided the resulting spacing does not exceed 16-3/4 inches (43 cm).

(7) Steps and rungs of ladder and stairway type access shall line up vertically with each other between rest platforms.

(8) Direct access to or from another surface shall be used only when the scaffold is not more than 14 inches (36 cm) horizontally and not more than 24 inches (61 cm) vertically from the other surface.

(9) Effective September 2, 1997, access for employees erecting or dismantling supported scaffolds shall be in accordance with the following:

(i) The employer shall provide safe means of access for each employee erecting or dismantling a scaffold where the provision of safe access is feasible and does not create a greater hazard. The employer shall have a competent person determine whether it is feasible or would pose a greater hazard to provide, and have employees use a safe means of access. This determination shall be based on site conditions and the type of scaffold being erected or dismantled.

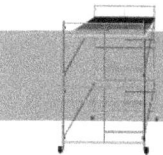

(1926.451(e) continued)

(ii) Hook-on or attachable ladders shall be installed as soon as scaffold erection has progressed to a point that permits safe installation and use.

(iii) When erecting or dismantling tubular welded frame scaffolds, (end) frames, with horizontal members that are parallel, level and are not more than 22 inches apart vertically may be used as climbing devices for access, provided they are erected in a manner that creates a usable ladder and provides good hand hold and foot space.

(iv) Cross braces on tubular welded frame scaffolds shall not be used as a means of access or egress.

(f) **Use.** (1) Scaffolds and scaffold components shall not be loaded in excess of their maximum intended loads or rated capacities, whichever is less.

(2) The use of shore or lean-to scaffolds is prohibited.

(3) Scaffolds and scaffold components shall be inspected for visible defects by a competent person before each work shift, and after any occurrence which could affect a scaffold's structural integrity.

(4) Any part of a scaffold damaged or weakened such that its strength is less than that required by paragraph (a) of this section shall be immediately repaired or replaced, braced to meet those provisions, or removed from service until repaired.

(5) Scaffolds shall not be moved horizontally while employees are on them, unless they have been designed by a registered professional engineer specifically for such movement or, for mobile scaffolds, where the provisions of §1926.452(w) are followed.

(6) The clearance between scaffolds and power lines shall be as follows: Scaffolds shall not be erected, used, dismantled, altered, or moved such that they or any conductive material handled on them might come closer to exposed and energized power lines than as follows:

Exception to paragraph (f)(6): Scaffolds and

Insulated Lines Voltage	Minimum Distance	Alternatives
Less than 300 volts 300 volts to 50 kv More than 50kv	3 feet (0.9 M) 10 feet (3.1 M) 10 feet (3.1 M) plus 0.4 inches (1.0 cm) for each 1 kv over 50 kv	2 times the length of the line insulator, but never less than 10 feet (3.1 m)

Uninsulated Lines Voltage	Minimum Distance	Alternatives
Less than 50 kv More than 50kv	10 feet (3.1 M) 10 feet (3.1 M) plus 0.4 inches (1.0 cm) for each 1 kv over 50 kv	2 times the length of the line insulator, but never less than 10 feet (3.1 m)

(1926.451(f) continued)

materials may be closer to power lines than specified above where such clearance is necessary for performance of work, and only after the utility company, or electrical system operator, has been notified of the need to work closer and the utility company, or electrical system operator, has deenergized the lines, relocated the lines, or installed protective coverings to prevent accidental contact with the lines.

(7) Scaffolds shall be erected, moved, dismantled, or altered only under the supervision and direction of a competent person qualified in scaffold erection, moving, dismantling or alteration. Such activities shall be performed only by experienced and trained employees selected for such work by the competent person.

(8) Employees shall be prohibited from working on scaffolds covered with snow, ice, or other slippery material except as necessary for removal of such materials.

(9) Where swinging loads are being hoisted onto or near scaffolds such that the loads might contact the scaffold, tag lines or equivalent measures to control the loads shall be used.

(10) Suspension ropes supporting adjustable suspension scaffolds shall be of a diameter large enough to provide sufficient surface area for the functioning of brake and hoist mechanisms.

(11) Suspension ropes shall be shielded from heat-producing processes. When acids or other corrosive substances are used on a scaffold, the ropes shall be shielded, treated to protect against the corrosive substances, or shall be of a material that will not be damaged by the substance being used.

(12) Work on or from scaffolds is prohibited during storms or high winds unless a competent person has determined that it is safe for employees to be on the scaffold and those employees are protected by a personal fall arrest system or wind screens. Wind screens shall not be used unless the scaffold is secured against the anticipated wind forces imposed.

(13) Debris shall not be allowed to accumulate on platforms.

(14) Makeshift devices, such as but not limited to boxes and barrels, shall not be used on top of scaffold platforms to increase the working level height of employees.

(15) Ladders shall not be used on scaffolds to increase the working level height of employees, except on large area scaffolds where employers have satisfied the following criteria:

(i) When the ladder is placed against a structure which is not a part of the scaffold, the scaffold shall be secured against the sideways thrust exerted by the ladder;

(ii) The platform units shall be secured to the scaffold to prevent their movement;

(iii) The ladder legs shall be on the same platform or other means shall be provided to stabilize the ladder against unequal platform deflection, and

(iv) The ladder legs shall be secured to prevent them from slipping or being pushed off the platform.

(16) Platforms shall not deflect more than 1/60 of the span when loaded.

(17) To reduce the possibility of welding current arcing through the suspension wire rope when performing welding from suspended scaffolds, the following precautions shall be taken, as applicable:

(i) An insulated thimble shall be used to attach each suspension wire rope to its hanging support (such as cornice hook or outrigger). Excess suspension wire rope and any additional independent lines from grounding shall be insulated;

(ii) The suspension wire rope shall be covered with insulating material extending at least 4 feet (1.2 m) above the hoist. If there is a tail line below the hoist, it shall be insulated to prevent contact with the platform. The portion of the tail line that hangs free below the scaffold shall be guided or retained, or both, so that it does not become grounded;

(iii) Each hoist shall be covered with insulated protective covers;

(iv) In addition to a work lead attachment required by the welding process, a grounding conductor shall be connected from the scaffold to the structure. The size of this conductor shall be at least the size of the welding process work lead, and this conductor shall not be in series with the welding process or the work piece;

(v) If the scaffold grounding lead is disconnected at any time, the welding machine shall be shut off; and

(vi) An active welding rod or uninsulated welding lead shall not be allowed to contact the scaffold or its suspension system.

(g) **Fall protection.** (1) Each employee on a scaffold more than 10 feet (3.1 m) above a lower

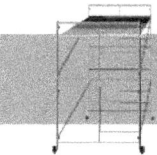

(1926.451(g) continued)

level shall be protected from falling to that lower level. Paragraphs (g)(1)(i) through (vii) of this section, establish the types of fall protection to be provided to the employees on each type of scaffold. Paragraph (g)(2) of this section addresses fall protection for scaffold erectors and dismantlers. NOTE to paragraph (g)(1): The fall protection requirements for employees installing suspension scaffold support systems on floors, roofs, and other elevated surfaces are set forth in subpart M of this part.

(i) Each employee on a boatswains' chair, catenary scaffold, float scaffold, needle beam scaffold, or ladder jack scaffold shall be protected by a personal fall arrest system;

(ii) Each employee on a single-point or two-point adjustable suspension scaffold shall be protected by both a personal fall arrest system and guardrail system;

(iii) Each employee on a crawling board (chicken ladder) shall be protected by a personal fall arrest system, a guardrail system (with minimum 200 pound toprail capacity), or by a three-fourth inch (1.9 cm) diameter grabline or equivalent handhold securely fastened beside each crawling board;

(iv) Each employee on a self-contained adjustable scaffold shall be protected by a guardrail system (with minimum 200 pound toprail capacity) when the platform is supported by the frame structure, and by both a personal fall arrest system and a guardrail system (with minimum 200 pound toprail capacity) when the platform is supported by ropes;

(v) Each employee on a walkway located within a scaffold shall be protected by a guardrail system (with minimum 200 pound toprail capacity) installed within 9 1/2 inches (24.1 cm) of and along at least one side of the walkway.

(vi) Each employee performing overhand bricklaying operations from a supported scaffold shall be protected from falling from all open sides and ends of the scaffold (except at the side next to the wall being laid) by the use of a personal fall arrest system or guardrail system (with minimum 200 pound toprail capacity).

(vii) For all scaffolds not otherwise specified in paragraphs (g)(1)(i) through (g)(1)(vi) of this section, each employee shall be protected by the use of personal fall arrest systems or guardrail

systems meeting the requirements of paragraph (g)(4) of this section.

(2) Effective September 2, 1997, the employer shall have a competent person determine the feasibility and safety of providing fall protection for employees erecting or dismantling supported scaffolds. Employers are required to provide fall protection for employees erecting or dismantling supported scaffolds where the installation and use of such protection is feasible and does not create a greater hazard.

(3) In addition to meeting the requirements of §1926.502(d), personal fall arrest systems used on scaffolds shall be attached by lanyard to a vertical lifeline, horizontal lifeline, or scaffold structural member. Vertical lifelines shall not be used when overhead components, such as overhead protection or additional platform levels, are part of a single-point or two-point adjustable suspension scaffold.

(i) When vertical lifelines are used, they shall be fastened to a fixed safe point of anchorage, shall be independent of the scaffold, and shall be protected from sharp edges and abrasion. Safe points of anchorage include structural members of buildings, but do not include standpipes, vents, other piping systems, electrical conduit, outrigger beams, or counterweights.

(ii) When horizontal lifelines are used, they shall be secured to two or more structural members of the scaffold, or they may be looped around both suspension and independent suspension lines (on scaffolds so equipped) above the hoist and brake attached to the end of the scaffold. Horizontal lifelines shall not be attached only to the suspension ropes.

(iii) When lanyards are connected to horizontal lifelines or structural members on a single-point or two-point adjustable suspension scaffold, the scaffold shall be equipped with additional independent support lines and automatic locking devices capable of stopping the fall of the scaffold in the event one or both of the suspension ropes fail. The independent support lines shall be equal in number and strength to the suspension ropes.

(iv) Vertical lifelines, independent support lines, and suspension ropes shall not be attached to each other, nor shall they be attached to or use the same point of anchorage, nor shall they be attached to the same point on the scaffold or personal fall arrest

(1926.451(g) continued)

system.

(4) Guardrail systems installed to meet the requirements of this section shall comply with the following provisions (guardrail systems built in accordance with Appendix A to this subpart will be deemed to meet the requirements of paragraphs (g)(4)(vii), (viii), and (ix) of this section):

(i) Guardrail systems shall be installed along all open sides and ends of platforms. Guardrail systems shall be installed before the scaffold is released for use by employees other than erection/dismantling crews.

(ii) The top edge height of toprails or equivalent member on supported scaffolds manufactured or placed in service after January 1, 2000 shall be installed between 38 inches (0.97 m) and 45 inches (1.2 m) above the platform surface. The top edge height on supported scaffolds manufactured and placed in service before January 1, 2000, and on all suspended scaffolds where both a guardrail and a personal fall arrest system are required shall be between 36 inches (0.9 m) and 45 inches (1.2 m). When conditions warrant, the height of the top edge may exceed the 45-inch height, provided the guardrail system meets all other criteria of paragraph (g)(4).

(iii) When midrails, screens, mesh, intermediate vertical members, solid panels, or equivalent structural members are used, they shall be installed between the top edge of the guardrail system and the scaffold platform.

(iv) When midrails are used, they shall be installed at a height approximately midway between the top edge of the guardrail system and the platform surface.

(v) When screens and mesh are used, they shall extend from the top edge of the guardrail system to the scaffold platform, and along the entire opening between the supports.

(vi) When intermediate members (such as balusters or additional rails) are used, they shall not be more than 19 inches (48 cm) apart.

(vii) Each toprail or equivalent member of a guardrail system shall be capable of withstanding, without failure, a force applied in any downward or horizontal direction at any point along its top edge of at least 100 pounds (445 n) for guardrail systems installed on single-point adjustable suspension scaffolds or two-point adjustable suspension scaffolds, and at least 200 pounds (890 n) for

guardrail systems installed on all other scaffolds.

(viii) When the loads specified in paragraph (g)(4)(vii) of this section are applied in a downward direction, the top edge shall not drop below the height above the platform surface that is prescribed in paragraph (g)(4)(ii) of this section.

(ix) Midrails, screens, mesh, intermediate vertical members, solid panels, and equivalent structural members of a guardrail system shall be capable of withstanding, without failure, a force applied in any downward or horizontal direction at any point along the midrail or other member of at least 75 pounds (333 n) for guardrail systems with a minimum 100 pound toprail capacity, and at least 150 pounds (666 n) for guardrail systems with a minimum 200 pound toprail capacity.

(x) Suspension scaffold hoists and non-walk-through stirrups may be used as end guardrails, if the space between the hoist or stirrup and the side guardrail or structure does not allow passage of an employee to the end of the scaffold.

(xi) Guardrails shall be surfaced to prevent injury to an employee from punctures or lacerations, and to prevent snagging of clothing.

(xii) The ends of all rails shall not overhang the terminal posts except when such overhang does not constitute a projection hazard to employees.

(xiii) Steel or plastic banding shall not be used as a toprail or midrail.

(xiv) Manila or plastic (or other synthetic) rope being used for toprails or midrails shall be inspected by a competent person as frequently as necessary to ensure that it continues to meet the strength requirements of paragraph (g) of this section.

(xv) Cross bracing is acceptable in place of a midrail when the crossing point of two braces is between 20 inches (0.5 m) and 30 inches (0.8 m) above the work platform or as a toprail when the crossing point of two braces is between 38 inches (0.97 m) and 48 inches (1.3 m) above the work platform. The end points at each upright shall be no more than 48 inches (1.3 m) apart.

(h) **Falling object protection.** (1) In addition to wearing hardhats each employee on a scaffold shall be provided with additional protection from falling hand tools, debris, and other small objects through the installation of toeboards, screens, or guardrail systems, or through the erection of debris nets, catch platforms, or canopy structures that contain or deflect the falling objects. When the

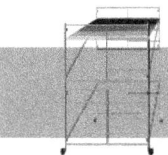
(1926.451(h) continued)

falling objects are too large, heavy or massive to be contained or deflected by any of the above-listed measures, the employer shall place such potential falling objects away from the edge of the surface from which they could fall and shall secure those materials as necessary to prevent their falling.

(2) Where there is a danger of tools, materials, or equipment falling from a scaffold and striking employees below, the following provisions apply:

(i) The area below the scaffold to which objects can fall shall be barricaded, and employees shall not be permitted to enter the hazard area; or

(ii) A toeboard shall be erected along the edge of platforms more than 10 feet (3.1 m) above lower levels for a distance sufficient to protect employees below, except on float (ship) scaffolds where an edging of 3/4 x 1-1/2 inch (2 x 4 cm) wood or equivalent may be used in lieu of toeboards;

(iii) Where tools, materials, or equipment are piled to a height higher than the top edge of the toeboard, paneling or screening extending from the toeboard or platform to the top of the guardrail shall be erected for a distance sufficient to protect employees below, or

(iv) A guardrail system shall be installed with openings small enough to prevent passage of potential falling objects, or

(v) A canopy structure, debris net, or catch platform strong enough to withstand the impact forces of the potential falling objects shall be erected over the employees below.

(3) Canopies, when used for falling object protection, shall comply with the following criteria:

(i) Canopies shall be installed between the falling object hazard and the employees.

(ii) When canopies are used on suspension scaffolds for falling object protection, the scaffold shall be equipped with additional independent support lines equal in number to the number of points supported, and equivalent in strength to the strength of the suspension ropes.

(iii) Independent support lines and suspension ropes shall not be attached to the same points of anchorage.

(4) Where used, toeboards shall be:

(i) Capable of withstanding, without failure, a force of at least 50 pounds (222 n) applied in any downward or horizontal direction at any point along the toeboard (toeboards built in accordance with Appendix A to this subpart will be deemed to meet this requirement); and

(ii) At least three and one-half inches (9 cm) high from the top edge of the toe board to the level of the walking/working surface. Toeboards shall be securely fastened in place at the outermost edge of the platform and have not more than 1/4 inch (0.7 cm) clearance above the walking/working surface. Toeboards shall be solid or with openings not over one inch (2.5 cm) in the greatest dimension.

§1926.452 Additional requirements applicable to specific types of scaffolds.

In addition to the applicable requirements of §1926.451, the following requirements apply to the specific types of scaffolds indicated. Scaffolds not specifically addressed by §1926.452, such as but not limited to systems scaffolds, must meet the requirements of §1926.451.

(a) **Pole scaffolds.** (1) When platforms are being moved to the next level, the existing platform shall be left undisturbed until the new bearers have been set in place and braced, prior to receiving the new platforms.

(2) Crossbracing shall be installed between the inner and outer sets of poles on double pole scaffolds.

(3) Diagonal bracing in both directions shall be installed across the entire inside face of double-pole scaffolds used to support loads equivalent to a uniformly distributed load of 50 pounds (222 kg) or more per square foot (929 square cm).

(4) Diagonal bracing in both directions shall be installed across the entire outside face of all double- and single-pole scaffolds.

(5) Runners and bearers shall be installed on edge.

(6) Bearers shall extend a minimum of 3 inches (7.6 cm) over the outside edges of runners.

(7) Runners shall extend over a minimum of two poles, and shall be supported by bearing blocks securely attached to the poles.

(8) Braces, bearers, and runners shall not be spliced between poles.

(9) Where wooden poles are spliced, the ends shall be squared and the upper section shall rest squarely on the lower section. Wood splice plates shall be provided on at least two adjacent sides, and shall extend at least 2 feet (0.6 m) on either side of the splice, overlap the abutted ends equally, and have at least the same cross-sectional areas as the pole. Splice plates of other materials of equivalent strength may be used.

(1926.452(a) continued)

(10) Pole scaffolds over 60 feet in height shall be designed by a registered professional engineer, and shall be constructed and loaded in accordance with that design. Non-mandatory Appendix A to this subpart contains examples of criteria that will enable an employer to comply with design and loading requirements for pole scaffolds under 60 feet in height.

(b) **Tube and coupler scaffolds.** (1) When platforms are being moved to the next level, the existing platform shall be left undisturbed until the new bearers have been set in place and braced prior to receiving the new platforms.

(2) Transverse bracing forming an "X" across the width of the scaffold shall be installed at the scaffold ends and at least at every third set of posts horizontally (measured from only one end) and every fourth runner vertically. Bracing shall extend diagonally from the inner or outer posts or runners upward to the next outer or inner posts or runners. Building ties shall be installed at the bearer levels between the transverse bracing and shall conform to the requirements of §1926.451(c)(1).

(3) On straight run scaffolds, longitudinal bracing across the inner and outer rows of posts shall be installed diagonally in both directions, and shall extend from the base of the end posts upward to the top of the scaffold at approximately a 45 degree angle. On scaffolds whose length is greater than their height, such bracing shall be repeated beginning at least at every fifth post. On scaffolds whose length is less than their height, such bracing shall be installed from the base of the end posts upward to the opposite end posts, and then in alternating directions until reaching the top of the scaffold. Bracing shall be installed as close as possible to the intersection of the bearer and post or runner and post.

(4) Where conditions preclude the attachment of bracing to posts, bracing shall be attached to the runners as close to the post as possible.

(5) Bearers shall be installed transversely between posts, and when coupled to the posts, shall have the inboard coupler bear directly on the runner coupler. When the bearers are coupled to the runners, the couplers shall be as close to the posts as possible.

(6) Bearers shall extend beyond the posts and runners, and shall provide full contact with the coupler.

(7) Runners shall be installed along the length of the scaffold, located on both the inside and outside posts at level heights (when tube and coupler guardrails and midrails are used on outside posts, they may be used in lieu of outside runners).

(8) Runners shall be interlocked on straight runs to form continuous lengths, and shall be coupled to each post. The bottom runners and bearers shall be located as close to the base as possible.

(9) Couplers shall be of a structural metal, such as drop-forged steel, malleable iron, or structural grade aluminum. The use of gray cast iron is prohibited.

(10) Tube and coupler scaffolds over 125 feet in height shall be designed by a registered professional engineer, and shall be constructed and loaded in accordance with such design. Non-mandatory Appendix A to this subpart contains examples of criteria that will enable an employer to comply with design and loading requirements for tube and coupler scaffolds under 125 feet in height.

(c) **Fabricated frame scaffolds (tubular welded frame scaffolds).**

(1) When moving platforms to the next level, the existing platform shall be left undisturbed until the new end frames have been set in place and braced prior to receiving the new platforms.

(2) Frames and panels shall be braced by cross, horizontal, or diagonal braces, or combination thereof, which secure vertical members together laterally. The cross braces shall be of such length as will automatically square and align vertical members so that the erected scaffold is always plumb, level, and square. All brace connections shall be secured.

(3) Frames and panels shall be joined together vertically by coupling or stacking pins or equivalent means.

(4) Where uplift can occur which would displace scaffold end frames or panels, the frames or panels shall be locked together vertically by pins or equivalent means.

(5) Brackets used to support cantilevered loads shall:

(i) be seated with side-brackets parallel to the frames and end-brackets at 90 degrees to the frames;

(ii) not be bent or twisted from these positions; and

(iii) be used only to support personnel, unless the scaffold has been designed for other loads by a

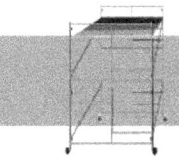

(1926.452(c) continued)

qualified engineer and built to withstand the tipping forces caused by those other loads being placed on the bracket-supported section of the scaffold.

(6) Scaffolds over 125 feet (38.0 m) in height above their base plates shall be designed by a registered professional engineer, and shall be constructed and loaded in accordance with such design.

(d) **Plasterers', decorators', and large area scaffolds.** Scaffolds shall be constructed in accordance with paragraphs (a), (b), or (c) of this section, as appropriate.

(e) **Bricklayers' square scaffolds (squares).**
(1) Scaffolds made of wood shall be reinforced with gussets on both sides of each corner.

(2) Diagonal braces shall be installed on all sides of each square.

(3) Diagonal braces shall be installed between squares on the rear and front sides of the scaffold, and shall extend from the bottom of each square to the top of the next square.

(4) Scaffolds shall not exceed three tiers in height, and shall be so constructed and arranged that one square rests directly above the other. The upper tiers shall stand on a continuous row of planks laid across the next lower tier, and shall be nailed down or otherwise secured to prevent displacement.

(f) **Horse scaffolds.** (1) Scaffolds shall not be constructed or arranged more than two tiers or 10 feet (3.0 m) in height, whichever is less.

(2) When horses are arranged in tiers, each horse shall be placed directly over the horse in the tier below.

(3) When horses are arranged in tiers, the legs of each horse shall be nailed down or otherwise secured to prevent displacement.

(4) When horses are arranged in tiers, each tier shall be crossbraced.

(g) **Form scaffolds and carpenters' bracket scaffolds.**
(1) Each bracket, except those for wooden bracket-form scaffolds, shall be attached to the supporting formwork or structure by means of one or more of the following: nails; a metal stud attachment device; welding; hooking over a secured structural supporting member, with the form wales either bolted to the form or secured by snap ties or tie bolts extending through the form and securely

anchored; or, for carpenters' bracket scaffolds only, by a bolt extending through to the opposite side of the structure's wall.

(2) Wooden bracket-form scaffolds shall be an integral part of the form panel.

(3) Folding type metal brackets, when extended for use, shall be either bolted or secured with a locking-type pin.

(h) **Roof bracket scaffolds.** (1) Scaffold brackets shall be constructed to fit the pitch of the roof and shall provide a level support for the platform.

(2) Brackets (including those provided with pointed metal projections) shall be anchored in place by nails unless it is impractical to use nails. When nails are not used, brackets shall be secured in place with first-grade manila rope of at least three-fourth inch (1.9 cm) diameter, or equivalent.

(i) **Outrigger scaffolds.** (1) The inboard end of outrigger beams, measured from the fulcrum point to the extreme point of anchorage, shall be not less than one and one-half times the outboard end in length.

(2) Outrigger beams fabricated in the shape of an I-beam or channel shall be placed so that the web section is vertical.

(3) The fulcrum point of outrigger beams shall rest on secure bearings at least 6 inches (15.2 cm) in each horizontal dimension.

(4) Outrigger beams shall be secured in place against movement, and shall be securely braced at the fulcrum point against tipping.

(5) The inboard ends of outrigger beams shall be securely anchored either by means of braced struts bearing against sills in contact with the overhead beams or ceiling, or by means of tension members secured to the floor joists underfoot, or by both.

(6) The entire supporting structure shall be securely braced to prevent any horizontal movement.

(7) To prevent their displacement, platform units shall be nailed, bolted, or otherwise secured to outriggers.

(8) Scaffolds and scaffold components shall be designed by a registered professional engineer and shall be constructed and loaded in accordance with such design.

(j) **Pump jack scaffolds.** (1) Pump jack brackets, braces, and accessories shall be fabricated from metal plates and angles. Each pump jack bracket shall have two positive gripping mechanisms to prevent any failure or slippage.

(1926.452(j) continued)

(2) Poles shall be secured to the structure by rigid triangular bracing or equivalent at the bottom, top, and other points as necessary. When the pump jack has to pass bracing already installed, an additional brace shall be installed approximately 4 feet (1.2 m) above the brace to be passed, and shall be left in place until the pump jack has been moved and the original brace reinstalled.

(3) When guardrails are used for fall protection, a workbench may be used as the toprail only if it meets all the requirements in paragraphs (g)(4)(ii), (vii), (viii), and (xiii) of §1926.451.

(4) Work benches shall not be used as scaffold platforms.

(5) When poles are made of wood, the pole lumber shall be straight-grained, free of shakes, large loose or dead knots, and other defects which might impair strength.

(6) When wood poles are constructed of two continuous lengths, they shall be joined together with the seam parallel to the bracket.

(7) When two by fours are spliced to make a pole, mending plates shall be installed at all splices to develop the full strength of the member.

(k) **Ladder jack scaffolds.** (1) Platforms shall not exceed a height of 20 feet (6.1 m).

(2) All ladders used to support ladder jack scaffolds shall meet the requirements of subpart X of this part—Stairways and Ladders, except that job-made ladders shall not be used to support ladder jack scaffolds.

(3) The ladder jack shall be so designed and constructed that it will bear on the side rails and ladder rungs or on the ladder rungs alone. If bearing on rungs only, the bearing area shall include a length of at least 10 inches (25.4 cm) on each rung.

(4) Ladders used to support ladder jacks shall be placed, fastened, or equipped with devices to prevent slipping.

(5) Scaffold platforms shall not be bridged one to another.

(l) **Window jack scaffolds.** (1) Scaffolds shall be securely attached to the window opening.

(2) Scaffolds shall be used only for the purpose of working at the window opening through which the jack is placed.

(3) Window jacks shall not be used to support planks placed between one window jack and another, or for other elements of scaffolding.

(m) **Crawling boards (chicken ladders).** (1) Crawling boards shall extend from the roof peak to the eaves when used in connection with roof construction, repair, or maintenance.

(2) Crawling boards shall be secured to the roof by ridge hooks or by means that meet equivalent criteria (e.g., strength and durability).

(n) **Step, platform, and trestle ladder scaffolds.** (1) Scaffold platforms shall not be placed any higher than the second highest rung or step of the ladder supporting the platform.

(2) All ladders used in conjunction with step, platform and trestle ladder scaffolds shall meet the pertinent requirements of subpart X of this part—Stairways and Ladders, except that job-made ladders shall not be used to support such scaffolds.

(3) Ladders used to support step, platform, and trestle ladder scaffolds shall be placed, fastened, or equipped with devices to prevent slipping.

(4) Scaffolds shall not be bridged one to another.

(o) **Single-point adjustable suspension scaffolds.** (1) When two single-point adjustable suspension scaffolds are combined to form a two-point adjustable suspension scaffold, the resulting two-point scaffold shall comply with the requirements for two-point adjustable suspension scaffolds in paragraph (p) of this section.

(2) The supporting rope between the scaffold and the suspension device shall be kept vertical unless all of the following conditions are met:

(i) The rigging has been designed by a qualified person, and

(ii) The scaffold is accessible to rescuers, and

(iii) The supporting rope is protected to ensure that it will not chafe at any point where a change in direction occurs, and

(iv) The scaffold is positioned so that swinging cannot bring the scaffold into contact with another surface.

(3) Boatswains' chair tackle shall consist of correct size ball bearings or bushed blocks containing safety hooks and properly "eye-spliced" minimum five-eighth (5/8) inch (1.6 cm) diameter first-grade manila rope, or other rope which will satisfy the criteria (e.g., strength and durability) of manila rope.

(4) Boatswains' chair seat slings shall be reeved through four corner holes in the seat; shall cross each other on the underside of the seat; and shall be rigged so as to prevent slippage which could cause an out-of-level condition.

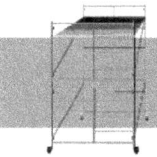

(1926.452(o) continued)

(5) Boatswains' chair seat slings shall be a minimum of five-eight (5/8) inch (1.6 cm) diameter fiber, synthetic, or other rope which will satisfy the criteria (e.g., strength, slip resistance, durability, etc.) of first grade manila rope.

(6) When a heat-producing process such as gas or arc welding is being conducted, boatswains' chair seat slings shall be a minimum of three-eight (3/8) inch (1.0 cm) wire rope.

(7) Non-cross-laminated wood boatswains' chairs shall be reinforced on their underside by cleats securely fastened to prevent the board from splitting.

(p) **Two-point adjustable suspension scaffolds (swing stages).** The following requirements do not apply to two-point adjustable suspension scaffolds used as masons' or stonesetters' scaffolds. Such scaffolds are covered by paragraph (q) of this section.

(1) Platforms shall not be more than 36 inches (0.9 m) wide unless designed by a qualified person to prevent unstable conditions.

(2) The platform shall be securely fastened to hangers (stirrups) by U-bolts or by other means which satisfy the requirements of §1926.451(a).

(3) The blocks for fiber or synthetic ropes shall consist of at least one double and one single block. The sheaves of all blocks shall fit the size of the rope used.

(4) Platforms shall be of the ladder-type, plank-type, beam-type, or light-metal type. Light metal-type platforms having a rated capacity of 750 pounds or less and platforms 40 feet (12.2 m) or less in length shall be tested and listed by a nationally recognized testing laboratory.

(5) Two-point scaffolds shall not be bridged or otherwise connected one to another during raising and lowering operations unless the bridge connections are articulated (attached), and the hoists properly sized.

(6) Passage may be made from one platform to another only when the platforms are at the same height, are abutting, and walk-through stirrups specifically designed for this purpose are used.

(q) **Multi-point adjustable suspension scaffolds, stonesetters' multi-point adjustable suspension scaffolds, and masons' multi-point adjustable suspension scaffolds.**

(1) When two or more scaffolds are used they shall not be bridged one to another unless they are designed to be bridged, the bridge connections are articulated, and the hoists are properly sized.

(2) If bridges are not used, passage may be made from one platform to another only when the platforms are at the same height and are abutting.

(3) Scaffolds shall be suspended from metal outriggers, brackets, wire rope slings, hooks, or means that meet equivalent criteria (e.g., strength, durability).

(r) **Catenary scaffolds.** (1) No more than one platform shall be placed between consecutive vertical pickups, and no more than two platforms shall be used on a catenary scaffold.

(2) Platforms supported by wire ropes shall have hook-shaped stops on each end of the platforms to prevent them from slipping off the wire ropes. These hooks shall be so placed that they will prevent the platform from falling if one of the horizontal wire ropes breaks.

(3) Wire ropes shall not be tightened to the extent that the application of a scaffold load will overstress them.

(4) Wire ropes shall be continuous and without splices between anchors.

(s) **Float (ship) scaffolds.** (1) The platform shall be supported by a minimum of two bearers, each of which shall project a minimum of 6 inches (15.2 cm) beyond the platform on both sides. Each bearer shall be securely fastened to the platform.

(2) Rope connections shall be such that the platform cannot shift or slip.

(3) When only two ropes are used with each float:

(i) They shall be arranged so as to provide four ends which are securely fastened to overhead supports.

(ii) Each supporting rope shall be hitched around one end of the bearer and pass under the platform to the other end of the bearer where it is hitched again, leaving sufficient rope at each end for the supporting ties.

(t) **Interior hung scaffolds.** (1) Scaffolds shall be suspended only from the roof structure or other structural member such as ceiling beams.

(2) Overhead supporting members (roof structure, ceiling beams, or other structural members) shall be inspected and checked for strength before the scaffold is erected.

(1926.452(t) continued)

(3) Suspension ropes and cables shall be connected to the overhead supporting members by shackles, clips, thimbles, or other means that meet equivalent criteria (e.g., strength, durability).

(u) **Needle beam scaffolds.** (1) Scaffold support beams shall be installed on edge.

(2) Ropes or hangers shall be used for supports, except that one end of a needle beam scaffold may be supported by a permanent structural member.

(3) The ropes shall be securely attached to the needle beams.

(4) The support connection shall be arranged so as to prevent the needle beam from rolling or becoming displaced.

(5) Platform units shall be securely attached to the needle beams by bolts or equivalent means. Cleats and overhang are not considered to be adequate means of attachment.

(v) **Multi-level suspended scaffolds.** (1) Scaffolds shall be equipped with additional independent support lines, equal in number to the number of points supported, and of equivalent strength to the suspension ropes, and rigged to support the scaffold in the event the suspension rope(s) fail.

(2) Independent support lines and suspension ropes shall not be attached to the same points of anchorage.

(3) Supports for platforms shall be attached directly to the support stirrup and not to any other platform.

(w) **Mobile scaffolds.** (1) Scaffolds shall be braced by cross, horizontal, or diagonal braces, or combination thereof, to prevent racking or collapse of the scaffold and to secure vertical members together laterally so as to automatically square and align the vertical members. Scaffolds shall be plumb, level, and squared. All brace connections shall be secured.

(i) Scaffolds constructed of tube and coupler components shall also comply with the requirements of paragraph (b) of this section;

(ii) Scaffolds constructed of fabricated frame components shall also comply with the requirements of paragraph (c) of this section.

(2) Scaffold casters and wheels shall be locked with positive wheel and/or wheel and swivel locks, or equivalent means, to prevent movement of the scaffold while the scaffold is used in a stationary manner.

(3) Manual force used to move the scaffold shall be applied as close to the base as practicable, but not more than 5 feet (1.5 m) above the supporting surface.

(4) Power systems used to propel mobile scaffolds shall be designed for such use. Forklifts, trucks, similar motor vehicles or add-on motors shall not be used to propel scaffolds unless the scaffold is designed for such propulsion systems.

(5) Scaffolds shall be stabilized to prevent tipping during movement.

(6) Employees shall not be allowed to ride on scaffolds unless the following conditions exist:

(i) The surface on which the scaffold is being moved is within 3 degrees of level, and free of pits, holes, and obstructions;

(ii) The height to base width ratio of the scaffold during movement is two to one or less, unless the scaffold is designed and constructed to meet or exceed nationally recognized stability test requirements such as those listed in paragraph (x) of Appendix A to this subpart (ANSI/SIA A92.5 and A92.6);

(iii) Outrigger frames, when used, are installed on both sides of the scaffold;

(iv) When power systems are used, the propelling force is applied directly to the wheels, and does not produce a speed in excess of 1 foot per second (.3 mps); and

(v) No employee is on any part of the scaffold which extends outward beyond the wheels, casters, or other supports.

(7) Platforms shall not extend outward beyond the base supports of the scaffold unless outrigger frames or equivalent devices are used to ensure stability.

(8) Where leveling of the scaffold is necessary, screw jacks or equivalent means shall be used.

(9) Caster stems and wheel stems shall be pinned or otherwise secured in scaffold legs or adjustment screws.

(10) Before a scaffold is moved, each employee on the scaffold shall be made aware of the move.

(x) **Repair bracket scaffolds.**

(1) Brackets shall be secured in place by at least one wire rope at least 1/2 inch (1.27 cm) in diameter.

(2) Each bracket shall be attached to the securing wire rope (or ropes) by a positive locking device capable of preventing the unintentional detachment of the bracket from the rope, or by equivalent means.

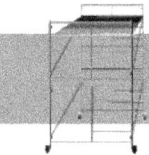

(1926.452(x) continued)

(3) Each bracket, at the contact point between the supporting structure and the bottom of the bracket, shall be provided with a shoe (heel block or foot) capable of preventing the lateral movement of the bracket.

(4) Platforms shall be secured to the brackets in a manner that will prevent the separation of the platforms from the brackets and the movement of the platforms or the brackets on a completed scaffold.

(5) When a wire rope is placed around the structure in order to provide a safe anchorage for personal fall arrest systems used by employees erecting or dismantling scaffolds, the wire rope shall meet the requirements of subpart M of this part, but shall be at least 5/16 inch (0.8 cm) in diameter.

(6) Each wire rope used for securing brackets in place or as an anchorage for personal fall arrest systems shall be protected from damage due to contact with edges, corners, protrusions, or other discontinuities of the supporting structure or scaffold components.

(7) Tensioning of each wire rope used for securing brackets in place or as an anchorage for personal fall arrest systems shall be by means of a turnbuckle at least 1 inch (2.54 cm) in diameter, or by equivalent means.

(8) Each turnbuckle shall be connected to the other end of its rope by use of an eyesplice thimble of a size appropriate to the turnbuckle to which it is attached.

(9) U-bolt wire rope clips shall not be used on any wire rope used to secure brackets or to serve as an anchor for personal fall arrest systems.

(10) The employer shall ensure that materials shall not be dropped to the outside of the supporting structure.

(11) Scaffold erection shall progress in only one direction around any structure.

(y) **Stilts**

Stilts, when used, shall be used in accordance with the following requirements:

(1) An employee may wear stilts on a scaffold only if it is a large area scaffold.

(2) When an employee is using stilts on a large area scaffold where a guardrail system is used to provide fall protection, the guardrail system shall be increased in height by an amount equal to the height of the stilts being used by the employee.

(3) Surfaces on which stilts are used shall be flat and free of pits, holes and obstructions, such as debris, as well as other tripping and falling hazards.

(4) Stilts shall be properly maintained. Any alteration of the original equipment shall be approved by the manufacturer.

1926.453 Aerial lifts.

(a) **General requirements.** (1) Unless otherwise provided in this section, aerial lifts acquired for use on or after January 22, 1973 shall be designed and constructed in conformance with the applicable requirements of the American National Standards for "Vehicle Mounted Elevating and Rotating Work Platforms," ANSI A92.2-1969, including appendix. Aerial lifts acquired before January 22, 1973, which do not meet the requirements of ANSI A92.2-1969, may not be used after January 1, 1976, unless they shall have been modified so as to conform with the applicable design and construction requirements of ANSI A92.2-1969. Aerial lifts include the following types of vehicle-mounted aerial devices used to elevate personnel to job-sites above ground: (i) Extensible boom platforms; (ii) aerial ladders; (iii) articulating boom platforms; (iv) vertical towers; and (v) a combination of any of this equipment. Aerial equipment may be made of metal, wood, fiberglass reinforced plastic (FRP), or other material; may be powered or manually operated; and are deemed to be aerial lifts whether or not they are capable of rotating about a substantially vertical axis.

(2) Aerial lifts may be "field modified" for uses other than those intended by the manufacturer provided the modification has been certified in writing by the manufacturer or by any other equivalent entity, such as a nationally recognized testing laboratory, to be in conformity with all applicable provisions of ANSI A92.2-1969 and this section and to be at least as safe as the equipment was before modification.

(b) **Specific requirements.** (1) Ladder trucks and tower trucks. Aerial ladders shall be secured in the lower traveling position by the locking device on top of the truck cab, and the manually operated device at the base of the ladder before the truck is moved for highway travel.

(2) Extensible and articulating boom platforms. (i) Lift controls shall be tested each day prior to use to determine that such controls are in safe working condition.

(1926.453(b) continued)

(ii) Only authorized persons shall operate an aerial lift.

(iii) Belting off to an adjacent pole, structure, or equipment while working from an aerial lift shall not be permitted.

(iv) Employees shall always stand firmly on the floor of the basket, and shall not sit or climb on the edge of the basket or use planks, ladders, or other devices for a work position.

(v) A body belt shall be worn and a lanyard attached to the boom or basket when working from an aerial lift.

(vi) Boom and basket load limits specified by the manufacturer shall not be exceeded.

(vii) The brakes shall be set and when outriggers are used, they shall be positioned on pads or a solid surface. Wheel chocks shall be installed before using an aerial lift on an incline, provided they can be safely installed.

(viii) An aerial lift truck shall not be moved when the boom is elevated in a working position with men in the basket, except for equipment which is specifically designed for this type of operation in accordance with the provisions of paragraphs (a)(1) and (2) of this section.

(ix) Articulating boom and extensible boom platforms, primarily designed as personnel carriers, shall have both platform (upper) and lower controls. Upper controls shall be in or beside the platform within easy reach of the operator. Lower controls shall provide for overriding the upper controls. Controls shall be plainly marked as to their function. Lower level controls shall not be operated unless permission has been obtained from the employee in the lift, except in case of emergency.

(x) Climbers shall not be worn while performing work from an aerial lift.

(xi) The insulated portion of an aerial lift shall not be altered in any manner that might reduce its insulating value.

(xii) Before moving an aerial lift for travel, the boom(s) shall be inspected to see that it is properly cradled and outriggers are in stowed position except as provided in paragraph (b)(2)(viii) of this section.

(3) Electrical tests. All electrical tests shall conform to the requirements of ANSI A92.2-1969 section 5. However equivalent d.c. voltage tests may be used in lieu of the a.c. voltage specified in A92.2-1969; d.c. voltage tests which are approved by the equipment manufacturer or equivalent entity shall be considered an equivalent test for the purpose of this paragraph (b)(3).

(4) Bursting safety factor. The provisions of the American National Standards Institute standard ANSI A92.2-1969, section 4.9 Bursting Safety Factor shall apply to all critical hydraulic and pneumatic components. Critical components are those in which a failure would result in a free fall or free rotation of the boom. All noncritical components shall have a bursting safety factor of at least 2 to 1.

(5) Welding standards. All welding shall conform to the following standards as applicable:

(i) Standard Qualification Procedure, AWS B 3.0-41.

(ii) Recommended Practices for Automotive Welding Design, AWS D8.4-61.

(iii) Standard Qualification of Welding Procedures and Welders for Piping and Tubing, AWS D10.9-69.

(iv) Specifications for Welding Highway and Railway Bridges, AWS D2.0-69.

NOTE to §1926.453: Non-mandatory Appendix C to this subpart lists examples of national consensus standards that are considered to provide employee protection equivalent to that provided through the application of ANSI A92.2-1969, where appropriate. This incorporation by reference was approved by the Director of the Federal Register in accordance with 5 U.S.C. 552(a) and 1 CFR part 51. Copies may be obtained from the American National Standards Institute. Copies may be inspected at the Docket Office, Occupational Safety and Health Administration, U.S. Department of Labor, 200 Constitution Avenue, NW., room N2634, Washington, DC or at the Office of the Federal Register, 800 North Capitol Street, NW., suite 700, Washington, DC.

§1926.454 Training requirements.

This section supplements and clarifies the requirements of §1926.21(b)(2) as these relate to the hazards of work on scaffolds.

(a) The employer shall have each employee who performs work while on a scaffold trained by a person qualified in the subject matter to recognize the hazards associated with the type of scaffold being used and to understand the procedures to control or minimize those hazards. The training shall include the following areas, as applicable:

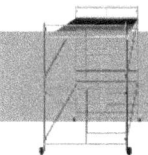

(1926.454(a) continued)

(1) The nature of any electrical hazards, fall hazards and falling object hazards in the work area;

(2) The correct procedures for dealing with electrical hazards and for erecting, maintaining, and disassembling the fall protection systems and falling object protection systems being used;

(3) The proper use of the scaffold, and the proper handling of materials on the scaffold;

(4) The maximum intended load and the load-carrying capacities of the scaffolds used; and

(5) Any other pertinent requirements of this subpart.

(b) The employer shall have each employee who is involved in erecting, disassembling, moving, operating, repairing, maintaining, or inspecting a scaffold trained by a competent person to recognize any hazards associated with the work in question. The training shall include the following topics, as applicable:

(1) The nature of scaffold hazards;

(2) The correct procedures for erecting, disassembling, moving, operating, repairing, inspecting, and maintaining the type of scaffold in question;

(3) The design criteria, maximum intended load-carrying capacity and intended use of the scaffold;

(4) Any other pertinent requirements of this subpart.

(c) When the employer has reason to believe that an employee lacks the skill or understanding needed for safe work involving the erection, use or dismantling of scaffolds, the employer shall retrain each such employee so that the requisite proficiency is regained. Retraining is required in at least the following situations:

(1) Where changes at the worksite present a hazard about which an employee has not been previously trained; or

(2) Where changes in the types of scaffolds, fall protection, falling object protection, or other equipment present a hazard about which an employee has not been previously trained; or

(3) Where inadequacies in an affected employee's work involving scaffolds indicate that the employee has not retained the requisite proficiency.

Non-Mandatory Appendices
Non-mandatory Appendix A to Subpart L — Scaffold Specifications

This Appendix provides non-mandatory guidelines to assist employers in complying with the requirements of subpart L of this part. An employer may use these guidelines and tables as a starting point for designing scaffold systems. However, the guidelines do not provide all the information necessary to build a complete system, and the employer is still responsible for designing and assembling these components in such a way that the completed system will meet the requirements of §1926.451(a). Scaffold components which are not selected and loaded in accordance with this Appendix, and components for which no specific guidelines or tables are given in this Appendix (e.g., joints, ties, components for wood pole scaffolds more than 60 feet in height, components for heavy-duty horse scaffolds, components made with other materials, and components with other dimensions, etc.) must be designed and constructed in accordance with the capacity requirements of §1926.451(a), and loaded in accordance with §1926.451(d)(1).

Index to Appendix A for Subpart L

1. General guidelines and tables.
2. Specific guidelines and tables.
   (a) Pole scaffolds:
      Single-pole wood pole scaffolds.
      Independent wood pole scaffolds.
   (c) Fabricated frame scaffolds.
   (d) Plasterers', decorators' and large area scaffolds.
   (e) Bricklayers' square scaffolds.
   (f) Horse scaffolds.
   (g) Form scaffolds and carpenters' bracket
   (h) Roof bracket scaffolds.
   (i) Outrigger scaffolds (one level).
   (j) Pump jack scaffolds.
   (l) Window jack scaffolds.
   (m)Crawling boards (chicken ladders).
   (n) Step, platform and trestle ladder scaffolds.
   (o) Single-point adjustable suspension scaffolds.
   (p) Two-point adjustable suspension scaffolds.
   (q)(1) Stonesetters' multi-point adjustable suspension scaffolds.
   (q)(2) Masons' multi-point adjustable suspension scaffolds.
   (r) Catenary scaffolds.

(Appendix A continued)

 (s) Float (ship) scaffolds.
 (t) Interior hung scaffolds.
 (u) Needle beam scaffolds.
 (v) Multi-level suspension scaffolds.
 (w) Mobile scaffolds.
 (x) Repair bracket scaffolds.
 (y) Stilts.
 (z) Tank builders' scaffolds.

1. General guidelines and tables.

 (a) The following tables, and the tables in Part 2—Specific guidelines and tables, assume that all load-carrying timber members (except planks) of the scaffold are a minimum of 1,500 lb-f/in^2 (stress grade) construction grade lumber. All dimensions are nominal sizes as provided in the American Softwood Lumber Standards, dated January 1970, except that, where rough sizes are noted, only rough or undressed lumber of the size specified will satisfy minimum requirements.

 (b) Solid sawn wood used as scaffold planks shall be selected for such use following the grading rules established by a recognized lumber grading association or by an independent lumber grading inspection agency. Such planks shall be identified by the grade stamp of such association or agency. The association or agency and the grading rules under which the wood is graded shall be certified by the Board of Review, American Lumber Standard Committee, as set forth in the American Softwood Lumber Standard of the U.S. Department of Commerce.

 Allowable spans shall be determined in compliance with the National Design Specification for Wood Construction published by the National Forest Products Association; paragraph 5 of ANSI A10.8-1988 Scaffolding-Safety Requirements published by the American National Standards Institute; or for 2 x 10 inch (nominal) or 2 x 9 inch (rough) solid sawn wood planks, as shown in the following table:

Maximum Intended Nominal Load (lb/ft^2)	Maximum Permissible Span Using Full Thickness Undressed Lumber (ft)	Maximum Permissible Span Using Nominal Thickness Lumber (ft)
25	10	8
50	8	6
75	6	–

 The maximum permissible span for 1-1/4 x 9-inch or wider wood plank of full thickness with a maximum intended load of 50 lb/ft^2 shall be 4 feet.

 (c) Fabricated planks and platforms may be used in lieu of solid sawn wood planks. Maximum spans for such units shall be as recommended by the manufacturer based on the maximum intended load being calculated as follows:

Rated Load Capacity	Intended Load
Light-duty	• 25 pounds per square foot applied uniformly over the entire span area.
Medium-duty	• 50 pounds per square foot applied uniformly over the entire span area.
Heavy-duty	• 75 pounds per square foot applied uniformly over the entire span area.
One-person	• 250 pounds placed at the center of the span (total 250 pounds).
Two-person	• 250 pounds placed 18 inches to the left and right of the center of the span (total 500 pounds).
Three-person	• 250 pounds placed at the center of the span and 250 pounds placed 18 inches to the left and right of the center of the span (total 750 pounds).

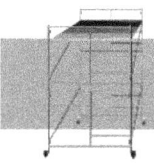

(Appendix A continued)

NOTE: Platform units used to make scaffold platforms intended for light-duty use shall be capable of supporting at least 25 pounds per square foot applied uniformly over the entire unit-span area, or a 250-pound point load placed on the unit at the center of the span, whichever load produces the greater shear force.

(d) Guardrails shall be as follows:

(i) Toprails shall be equivalent in strength to 2 inch by 4 inch lumber; or
1-1/4 inch x 1/8 inch structural angle iron; or
1 inch x .070 inch wall steel tubing; or 1.990 inch x .058 inch wall aluminum tubing.

(ii) Midrails shall be equivalent in strength to 1 inch by 6 inch lumber; or
1-1/4 inch x 1-1/4 inch x 1/8 inch structural angle iron; or
1 inch x .070 inch wall steel tubing; or
1.990 inch x .058 inch wall aluminum tubing.

(iii) Toeboards shall be equivalent in strength to 1 inch by 4 inch lumber; or
1-1/4 inch x 1-1/4 inch structural angle iron; or
1 inch x .070 inch wall steel tubing; or
1.990 inch x .058 inch wall aluminum tubing.

(iv) Posts shall be equivalent in strength to 2 inch by 4 inch lumber; or
1-1/4 inch x 1-1/4 inch x 1/8 structural angle iron; or
1 inch x .070 inch wall steel tubing; or
1.990 inch x .058 inch wall aluminum tubing.

(v) Distance between posts shall not exceed 8 feet.

(e) Overhead protection shall consist of 2 inch nominal planking laid tight, or 3/4-inch plywood.

(f) Screen installed between toeboards and midrails or toprails shall consist of No. 18 gauge U.S. Standard wire one inch mesh.

(Appendix A continued)
2. Specific guidelines and tables.
(a) Pole Scaffolds.

Single Pole Wood Pole Scaffolds

	Light Duty up to 20 feet High	Light Duty up to 60 feet High	Medium Duty up to 60 feet High	Heavy Duty up to 60 feet High
Maximum intended load	25 lbs/ft^2	25 lbs/ft^2	50 lbs/ft^2	75 lbs/ft^2
Poles or uprights	2 x 4 in.	4 x 4 in.	4 x 4 in.	4 x 6 in.
Maximum pole spacing (longitudinal)	6 feet	10 feet	8 feet	6 feet
Maximum pole spacing (transverse)	5 feet	5 feet	5 feet	5 feet
Runners	1 x 4 in.	1-1/4 x 9 in.	2 x 10 in.	2 x 10 in.
Bearers and maximum spacing of bearers: 3 feet	2 x 4 in.	2 x 4 in.	2 x 10 in. or 3 x 4 in.	2 x 10 in. or 3 x 5 in.
5 feet	2 x 6 in. or 3 x 4 in.	2 x 6 in. or 3 x 4 in. (rough)	2 x 10 in. or 3 x 4 in.	2 x 10 in. or 3 x 5 in.
6 feet	—	—	2 x 10 in. or 3 x 4 in. 2 x 10 in. or	2 x 10 in. or 3 x 5 in.
8 feet	—	—	3 x 4 in.	—
Planking	1-1/4 x 9 in.	2 x 10 in.	2 x 10 in.	2 x 10 in.
Maximum vertical spacing of horizontal members	7 feet	9 feet	7 feet	6 ft. 6 in.
Bracing horizontal	1 x 4 in.	1 x 4 in.	1 x 6 in. or 1-1/4 x 4 in.	2 x 4 in.
Bracing diagonal	1 x 4 in.	1 x 4 in.	1 x 4 in.	2 x 4 in.
Tie-ins	1 x 4 in.	1 x 4 in.	1 x 4 in.	1 x 4 in.

NOTE: All members except planking are used on edge. All wood bearers shall be reinforced with 3/16 x 2 inch steel strip, or the equivalent, secured to the lower edges for the entire length of the bearer.

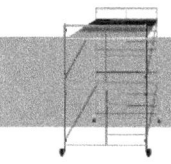

(Appendix A continued)

Independent Wood Pole Scaffolds

	Light Duty up to 20 feet High	Light Duty up to 60 feet High	Medium Duty up to 60 feet High	Heavy Duty up to 60 feet High
Maximum intended load	25 lbs/ft^2	25 lbs/ft^2	50 lbs/ft^2	75 lbs/ft^2
Poles or uprights	2 x 4 in.	4 x 4 in.	4 x 4 in.	4 x 4 in.
Maximum pole spacing (longitudinal)	6 feet	10 feet	8 feet	6 feet
Maximum (transverse)	6 feet	10 feet	8 feet	8 feet
Runners	1-1/4 x 4 in.	1-1/4 x 9 in.	2 x 10 in.	2 x 10 in.
Bearers and maximum spacing of bearers: 3 feet	2 x 4 in	2 x 4 in.	2 x 10 in.	2 x 10 in. (rough)
6 feet	2 x 6 in. or 3 x 4 in.	2 x 10 in. (rough) or 3 x 8 in.	2 X 10 in.	2 x 10 in. or (rough)
8 feet	2 x 6 in. or 3 x 4 in.	2 x 10 in. (rough) or 3 x 8 in.	2 x 10 in.	—
10 feet	2 x 6 in. or 3 x 4 in.	2 x 10 in. (rough) or 3 x 3 in.	—	—
Planking	1-1/4 x 9 in.	2 x 10 in.	2 x 10 in.	2 x 10 in.
Maximum vertical spacing of horizontal members	7 feet	7 feet	6 feet	6 feet
Bracing horizontal	1 x 4 in.	1 x 4 in.	1 x 6 in. or 1-1/4 x 4 in.	2 x 4 in.
Bracing diagonal	1 x 4 in.	1 x 4 in.	1 x 4 in.	2 x 4 in.
Tie-ins	1 x 4 in.	1 x 4 in.	1 x 4 in.	1 x 4 in.

NOTE: All members except planking are used on edge. All wood bearers shall be reinforced with 3/16 x 2 inch steel strip, or the equivalent, secured to the lower edges for the entire length of the bearer.

(Appendix A continued)

(b) Tube and coupler scaffolds.

Minimum Size of Members

	Light Duty	Medium Duty	Heavy Duty
Maximum intended load	25 lbs/ft²	50 lbs/ft²	75 lbs/ft²
Posts, runners, and braces	Nominal 2 in. (1.90 inches) OD steel tube or pipe	Nominal 2 in. (1.90 inches) OD steel tube or pipe	Nominal 2 in. (1.90 inches) OD steel tube or pipe
Bearers	Nominal 2 in. (1.90 inches) OD steel tube or pipe and a maximum post spacing of 4 ft. x 10 ft.*	Nominal 2 in. (1.90 inches) OD steel tube or pipe and a maximum post spacing of 4 ft. x 7 ft. or Nominal 2-1/2 in. (2.375 in.) OD steel tube or pipe and a maximum post spacing of 6 ft. x 8 ft.*	Nominal 2-1/2 in. (2.375 in.) OD steel tube or pipe and a maximum post spacing of 6 ft. x 6 ft.
Maximum runner spacing vertically	6 ft. 6 in.	6 ft. 6 in.	6 ft. 6 in.

Bearers shall be installed in the direction of the shorter dimension.

NOTE: Longitudinal diagonal bracing shall be installed at an angle of 45° (± 5°).

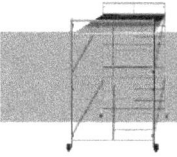

(Appendix A continued)

Maximum Number of Planked Levels

	Maximum Number of Additional Planked Levels			Maximum Height of Scaffold (in feet)
	Light Duty	Medium Duty	Heavy Duty	
Number of Working Levels				
1	16	11	6	125
2	11	1	0	125
3	6	0	0	125
4	1	0	0	125

(c) *Fabricated frame scaffolds.* Because of their prefabricated nature,
no additional guidelines or tables for these scaffolds are being adopted in this
Appendix.

(d) *Plasterers', decorators', and large area scaffolds.* The guidelines for pole scaffolds or tube and coupler scaffolds (Appendix A(a) and (b)) may be applied.

(e) *Bricklayers' square scaffolds.*

Maximum intended load	50 lb/ft 2*
Maximum width	5 ft
Maximum height	5 ft
Gussets	1 x 6 in
Braces	1 x 8 in
Legs	2 x 6 in
Bearers (horizontal members)	2 x 6 in

*The squares shall be set not more than 8 feet apart for light duty scaffolds and not
more than 5 feet apart for medium duty scaffolds.

(f) *Horse scaffolds.*

Maximum intended load (light duty)	25 lb/ft 2*
Maximum intended load (medium duty)	50 lb/ft 2*

Horizontal members or bearers:

Light duty	2 x 4 in
Medium duty	3 x 4 in
Legs	2 x 4 in
Longitudinal brace between legs	1 x 6 in
Gusset brace at top of legs	1 x 8 in
Half diagonal braces	2 x 4 in

*Horses shall be spaced not more than 8 feet apart for light duty loads, and not more than 5 feet apart for medium duty loads.

(g) *Form scaffolds and carpenters' bracket scaffolds.*

(1) Brackets shall consist of a triangular-shaped frame made of wood with a cross-section not less than 2 inches by 3 inches, or of 1-1/4 inch x 1-1/4 inch x 1/8 inch structural angle iron.

(2) Bolts used to attach brackets to structures shall not be less than 5/8 inches in diameter.

(3) Maximum bracket spacing shall be 8 feet on centers.

(4) No more than two employees shall occupy any given 8 feet of a bracket or form scaffold at any one time.
Tools and materials shall not exceed 75 pounds in addition to the occupancy.

(5) Wooden figure-four scaffolds:

Maximum intended load	25 lb/ft 2
Uprights	2 x 4 in or 2 x 6 in
Bearers (two)	1 x 6 in
Braces	1 x 6 in
Maximum length of bearers (unsupported)	3 ft - 6 in

(i) Outrigger bearers shall consist of two pieces of 1 x 6 inch lumber nailed on opposite sides of the vertical support.

(ii) Bearers for wood figure-four brackets shall project not more than 3 feet 6 inches from the outside of the form support, and shall be braced and secured to prevent tipping or turning. The knee or angle brace shall intersect the bearer at least 3 feet from the form at an angle of approximately 45 degrees, and the lower end shall be nailed to a vertical support.

(Appendix A continued)

(6) Metal bracket scaffolds:

Maximum intended load	25 lb/ft ^{2}
Uprights	2 x 4 inch
Bearers	As designed
Braces	As designed

(7) Wood bracket scaffolds:

Maximum intended load	25 lb/ft ^{2}
Uprights	2 x 4 in or 2 x 6 in
Bearers	2 x 6 in
Maximum scaffold width	3 ft 6 in
Braces	1 x 6 in

(h) *Roof bracket scaffolds.* No specific guidelines or tables are given.

(i) *Outrigger scaffolds (single level).* No specific guidelines or tables are given.

(j) *Pump jack scaffolds.* Wood poles shall not exceed 30 feet in height. Maximum intended load— 500 lbs between poles; applied at the center of the span. Not more than two employees shall be on a pump jack scaffold at one time between any two supports. When 2 x 4's are spliced together to make a 4 x 4 inch wood pole, they shall be spliced with "10 penny" common nails no more than 12 inches center to center, staggered uniformly from the opposite outside edges.

(k) *Ladder jack scaffolds.* Maximum intended load—25 lb/ft ^{2}. However, not more than two employees shall occupy any platform at any one time. Maximum span between supports shall be 8 feet.

(l) *Window jack scaffolds.* Not more than one employee shall occupy a window jack scaffold at any one time.

(m) *Crawling boards (chicken ladders).* Crawling boards shall be not less than 10 inches wide and 1 inch thick, with cleats having a minimum 1 x 1-1/2 inch cross-sectional area. The cleats shall be equal in length to the width of the board and spaced at equal intervals not to exceed 24 inches.

(n) *Step, platform, and trestle ladder scaffolds.* No additional guidelines or tables are given.

(o) *Single-point adjustable suspension scaffolds.* Maximum intended load—250 lbs.

Wood seats for boatswains' chairs shall be not less than 1 inch thick if made of non-laminated wood, or 5/8 inches thick if made of marine quality plywood.

(p) *Two-point adjustable suspension scaffolds.* (1) In addition to direct connections to buildings (except window cleaners' anchors) acceptable ways to prevent scaffold sway include angulated roping and static lines. Angulated roping is a system of platform suspension in which the upper wire rope sheaves or suspension points are closer to the plane of the building face than the corresponding attachment points on the platform, thus causing the platform to press against the face of the building. Static lines are separate ropes secured at their top and bottom ends closer to the plane of the building face than the outermost edge of the platform. By drawing the static line taut, the platform is drawn against the face of the building.

(2) On suspension scaffolds designed for a working load of 500 pounds, no more than two employees shall be permitted on the scaffold at one time. On suspension scaffolds with a working load of 750 pounds, no more than three employees shall be permitted on the scaffold at one time.

(3) Ladder-type platforms. The side stringer shall be of clear straight-grained spruce. The rungs shall be of straight-grained oak, ash, or hickory, at least 1-1/8 inches in diameter, with 7/8 inch tenons mortised into the side stringers at least 7/8 inch. The stringers shall be tied together with tie rods not less than 1/4 inch in diameter, passing through the stringers and riveted up tight against washers on both ends. The flooring strips shall be spaced not more than 5/8 inch apart, except at the side rails where the space may be 1 inch. Ladder-type platforms shall be constructed in accordance with the following table:

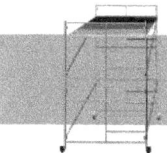

(Appendix A continued)

Schedule for Ladder-Type Platforms

Length of Platform	12 feet	14 & 16 feet	18 & 20 feet
Side stringers, minimum cross section (finished sizes):			
at ends	1-3/4 x 2-3/4 in.	1-3/4 x 2-3/4 in.	1-3/4 x 3 in.
at middle	1-3/4 x 3-3/4 in.	1-3/4 x 3-3/4 in.	1-3/4 x 4 in.
Reinforcing strip (minimum)	A 1/8 x 7/8 inch steel reinforcing strip shall be attached to the side or underside, full length. Rungs shall be 1-1/8 inch minimum diameter with a least 7/8 inch in diameter tenons, and the maximum spacing shall be 12 inches to center.		
Tie rods:			
Number (minimum)	3	4	4
Diameter (minimum)	1/4 in.	1/4 in.	1/4 in.
Flooring, minimum finished size	1/2 x 2-3/4 in.	1/2 x 2-3/4 in.	1/2 x 2-3/4 in.

Schedule for Ladder-Type Platforms

Length of Platform:	22 & 24 ft	28 & 30 ft.
Side stringers, minimum cross section (finished sizes):		
at ends	1-3/4 x 3 in.	1-3/4 x 3-1/2 in.
at middle	1-3/4 x 4-1/4 in.	1-3/4 x 5 in.
Reinforcing strip (minimum)	A 1/8 x 7/8-inch steel reinforcing strip shall be attached to the side or under side, full length.	
Rungs	Rungs shall be 1-1/8 inch minimum diameter with at least 7/8 inch in diameter tenons, and the maximum spacing shall be 12 inches to center. Tie rods	
Number (minimum)	5	6
Diameter (minimum)	1/4 in.	1/4 in.
Flooring, minimum finished size	1/2 x 2-3/4 in.	1/2 x 2-3/4 in.

(Appendix A continued)

(4) Plank-Type Platforms. Plank-type platforms shall be composed of not less than nominal 2 x 8 inch unspliced planks, connected together on the underside with cleats at intervals not exceeding 4 feet, starting 6 inches from each end. A bar or other effective means shall be securely fastened to the platform at each end to prevent the platform from slipping off the hanger. The span between hangers for plank-type platforms shall not exceed 10 feet.

(5) Beam-Type Platforms. Beam platforms shall have side stringers of lumber not less than 2 x 6 inches set on edge. The span between hangers shall not exceed 12 feet when beam platforms are used. The flooring shall be supported on 2 x 6 inch cross beams, laid flat and set into the upper edge of the stringers with a snug fit, at intervals of not more than 4 feet, securely nailed to the cross beams. Floor-boards shall not be spaced more than 1/2 inch apart.

(q)(1) *Multi-point adjustable suspension scaffolds and stonesetters' multi-point adjustable suspension scaffolds.* No specific guidelines or tables are given for these scaffolds.

(q)(2) *Masons' multi-point adjustable suspension scaffolds.* Maximum intended load—50 lb/ft². Each outrigger beam shall be at least a standard 7 inch, 15.3 pound steel I-beam, at least 15 feet long. Such beams shall not project more than 6 feet 6 inches beyond the bearing point. Where the overhang exceeds 6 feet 6 inches, outrigger beams shall be composed of stronger beams or multiple beams.

(r) *Catenary scaffolds.* (1) Maximum intended load -500 lbs.

(2) Not more than two employees shall be permitted on the scaffold at one time.

(3) Maximum capacity of come-along shall be 2,000 lbs.

(4) Vertical pickups shall be spaced not more than 50 feet apart.

(5) Ropes shall be equivalent in strength to at least 1/2 inch (1.3 cm) diameter improved plow steel wire rope.

(s) *Float (ship) scaffolds.* (1) Maximum intended load — 750 lbs.

(2) Platforms shall be made of 3/4 inch plywood, equivalent in rating to American Plywood Association Grade B-B, Group I, Exterior.

(3) Bearers shall be made from 2 x 4 inch, or 1 x 10 inch rough lumber. They shall be free of knots and other flaws.

(4) Ropes shall be equivalent in strength to at least 1 inch (2.5 cm) diameter first grade manila rope.

(t) *Interior hung scaffolds.*
Bearers (use on edge)   2 x 10 in
  Maximum intended load
Maximum span

25 lb/ft²	10 ft
50 lb/ft²	10 ft
75 lb/ft²	7 ft

(u) *Needle beam scaffolds*

Maximum intended load	25 lb/ft²
Beams	4 x 6 in
Maximum platform span	8 ft
Maximum beam span	10 ft

(1) Ropes shall be attached to the needle beams by a scaffold hitch or an eye splice. The loose end of the rope shall be tied by a bowline knot or by a round turn and a half hitch.

(2) Ropes shall be equivalent in strength to at least 1 inch (2.5 cm) diameter first grade manila rope.

(v) *Multi-level suspension scaffolds.* No additional guidelines or tables are being given for these scaffolds.

(w) *Mobile Scaffolds.* Stability test as described in the ANSI A92 series documents, as appropriate for the type of scaffold, can be used to establish stability for the purpose of §1926.452(w)(6).

(x) *Repair bracket scaffolds.* No additional guidelines or tables are being given for these scaffolds.

(y) *Stilts.* No specific guidelines or tables are given.

(z) *Tank builder's scaffold.*

(1) The maximum distance between brackets to which scaffolding and guardrail supports are attached shall be no more than 10 feet 6 inches.

(2) Not more than three employees shall occupy a 10 feet 6 inch span of scaffold planking at any time.

(3) A taut wire or synthetic rope supported on the scaffold brackets shall be installed at the scaffold plank level between the innermost edge of the scaffold platform and the curved plate structure of the tank shell to serve as a safety line in lieu of an inner guardrail assembly where the space between the scaffold platform and the tank exceeds 12 inches (30.48 cm). In the event the open space on either side of the rope exceeds 12 inches (30.48 cm), a second wire or synthetic rope appropriately placed, or guardrails in accordance with §1926.451(e)(4),

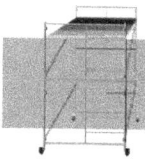
(Appendix A continued)

shall be installed in order to reduce that open space to less than 12 inches (30.48 cm).

(4) Scaffold planks of rough full-dimensioned 2-inch (5.1 cm) x 12-inch(30.5 cm) Douglas Fir or Southern Yellow Pine of Select Structural Grade shall be used. Douglas Fir planks shall have a fiber stress of at least 1900 lb/in² (130,929 n/cm²) and a modulus of elasticity of at least 1,900,000 lb/in² (130,929,000 n/cm²), while Yellow Pine planks shall have a fiber stress of at least 2500 lb/in² (172,275 n/cm²) and a modulus of elasticity of at least 2,000,000 lb/in² (137,820,000 n/cm²).

(5) Guardrails shall be constructed of a taut wire or synthetic rope, and shall be supported by angle irons attached to brackets welded to the steel plates. These guardrails shall comply with §1926.451(e)(4). Guardrail supports shall be located at no greater than 10 feet 6 inch intervals.

Non-mandatory Appendix B to Subpart L—Criteria for Determining the Feasibility of Providing Safe Access and Fall Protection for Scaffold Erectors and Dismantlers.

[Reserved]

Non-mandatory Appendix C to Subpart L—List of National Consensus Standards.

ANSI/SIA A92.2-1990 Vehicle-Mounted Elevating and RotatingAerial Devices

ANSI/SIA A92.3-1990 Manually Propelled Elevating Aerial Platforms

ANSI/SIA A92.5-1990 Boom Supported Elevating Work Platforms

ANSI/SIA A92.6-1990 Self-Propelled Elevating Work Platforms

ANSI/SIA A92.7-1990 Airline Ground Support Vehicle-Mounted Vertical Lift Devices

ANSI/SIA A92.8-1993 Vehicle-Mounted Bridge Inspection and Maintenance Devices

ANSI/SIA A92.9-1993 Mast-Climbing Work Platforms

Non-mandatory Appendix D to Subpart L—List of Training Topics for Scaffold Erectors and Dismantlers.

This Appendix D is provided to serve as a guide to assist employers when evaluating the training needs of employees erecting or dismantling supported scaffolds.

The Agency believes that employees erecting or dismantling scaffolds should be trained in the following topics:

• General Overview of Scaffolding
  • regulations and standards
  • erection/dismantling planning
  • PPE and proper procedures
  • fall protection
  • materials handling
  • access
  • working platforms
  • foundations
  • guys, ties and braces
• Tubular Welded Frame Scaffolds
  • specific regulations and standards
  • components
  • parts inspection
  • erection/dismantling planning
  • guys, ties and braces
  • fall protection
  • general safety
  • access and platforms
  • erection/dismantling procedures
  • rolling scaffold assembly
  • putlogs
• Tube and Clamp Scaffolds
  • specific regulations and standards
  • components
  • parts inspection
  • erection/dismantling planning
  • guys, ties and braces
  • fall protection
  • general safety
  • access and platforms
  • erection/dismantling procedures
  • buttresses, cantilevers, and bridges

(Appendix D continued)

• System scaffolds
  • specific regulations and standards
  • components
  • parts inspection
  • erection/dismantling planning
  • guys, ties and braces
  • fall protection
  • general safety
  • access and platforms
  • erection/dismantling procedures
  • buttresses, cantilevers, and bridges

Scaffold erectors and dismantlers should all receive the general overview, in addition to specific training for the type of supported scaffold being erected or dismantled.

Non-mandatory Appendix E to Subpart L— Drawings and Illustrations

This Appendix provides drawings of particular types of scaffolds and scaffold components, and graphic illustrations of bracing patterns and tie spacing patterns.

This Appendix is intended to provide visual guidance to assist the user in complying with the requirements of subpart L, part 1926.

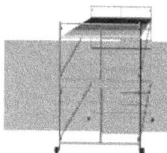

(Appendix E continued)

BRACING – TUBE & COUPLER SCAFFOLDS

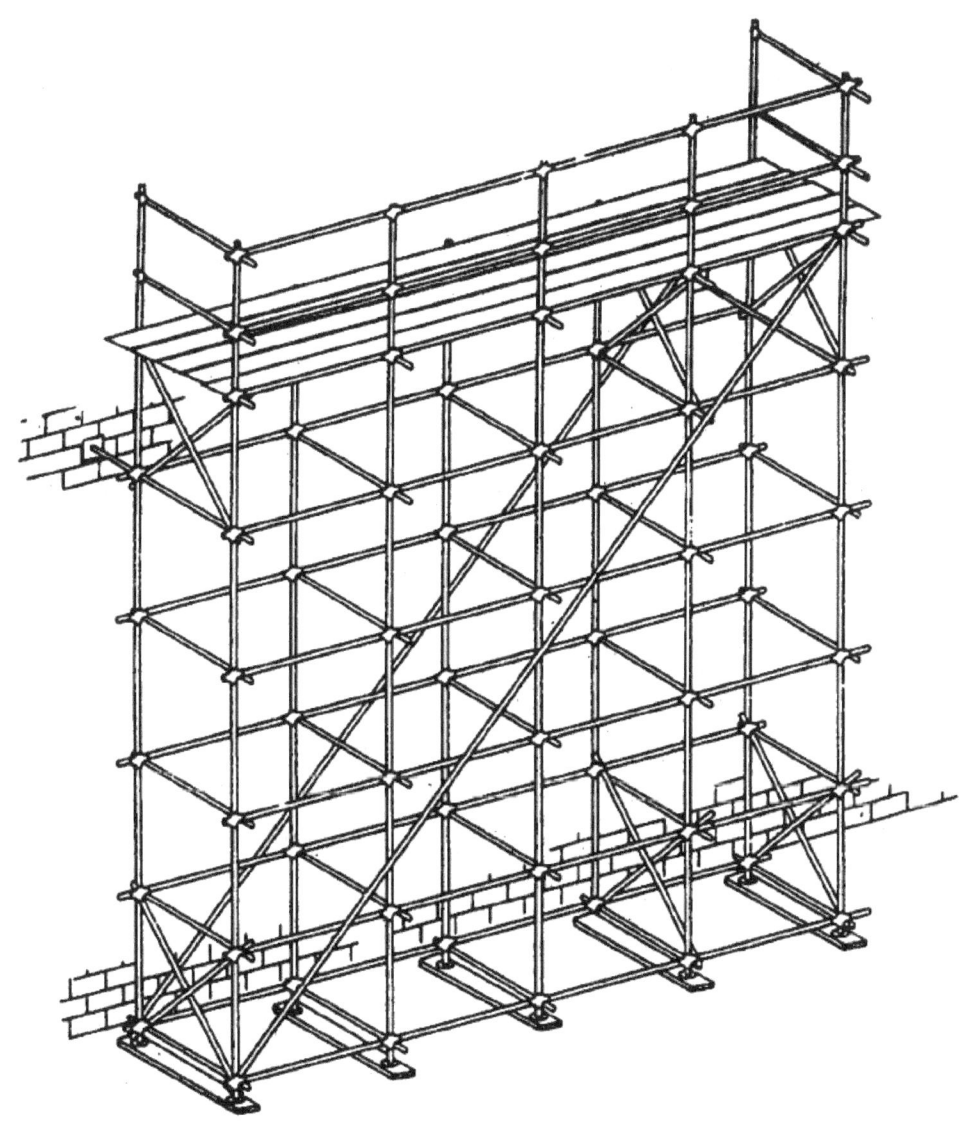

(Appendix E continued)

SUSPENDED SCAFFOLD PLATFORM WELDING PRECAUTIONS

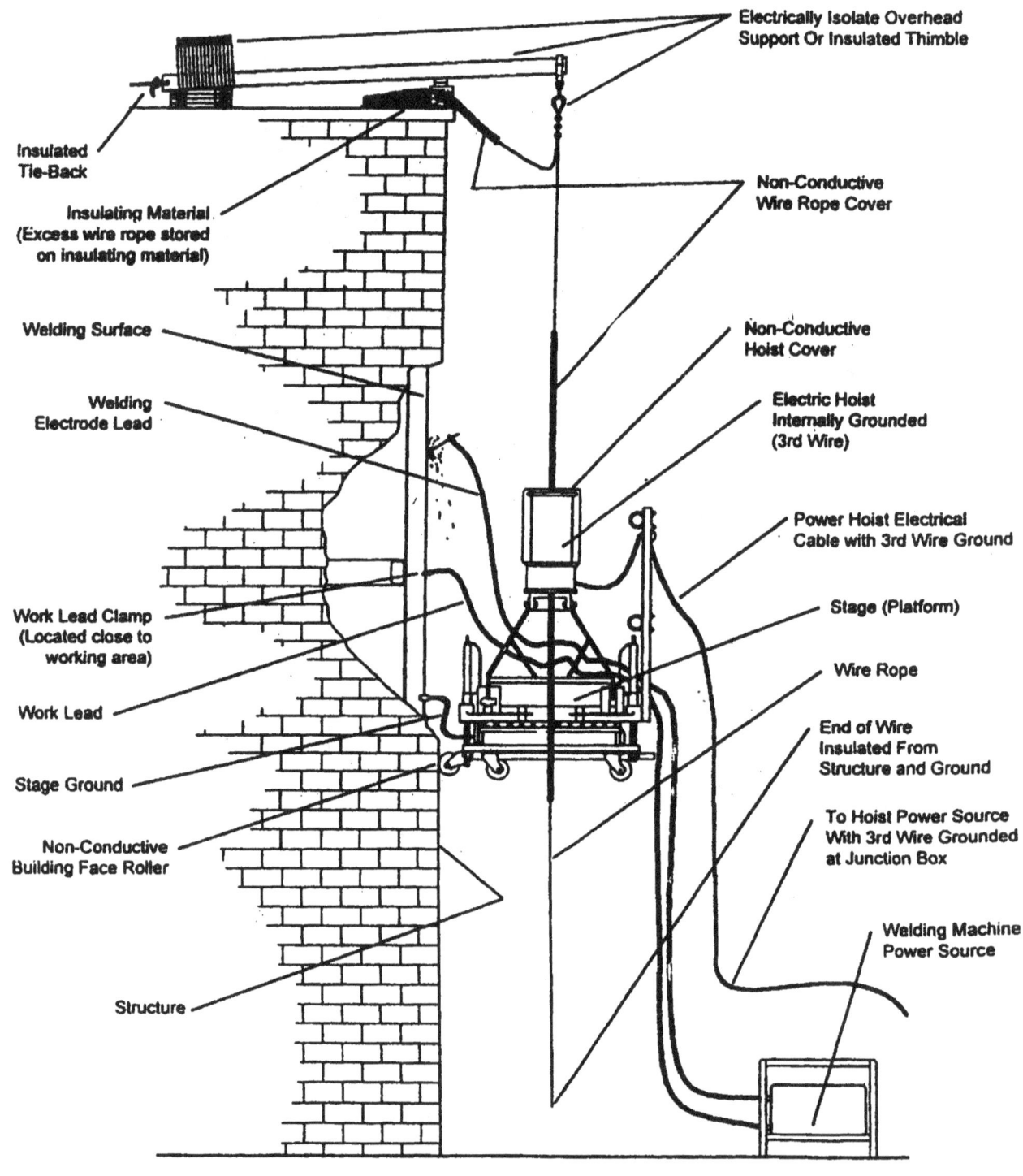

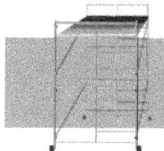

(Appendix E continued)

MAXIMUM VERTICAL TIE SPACING
WIDER THAN 3'-0" BASES

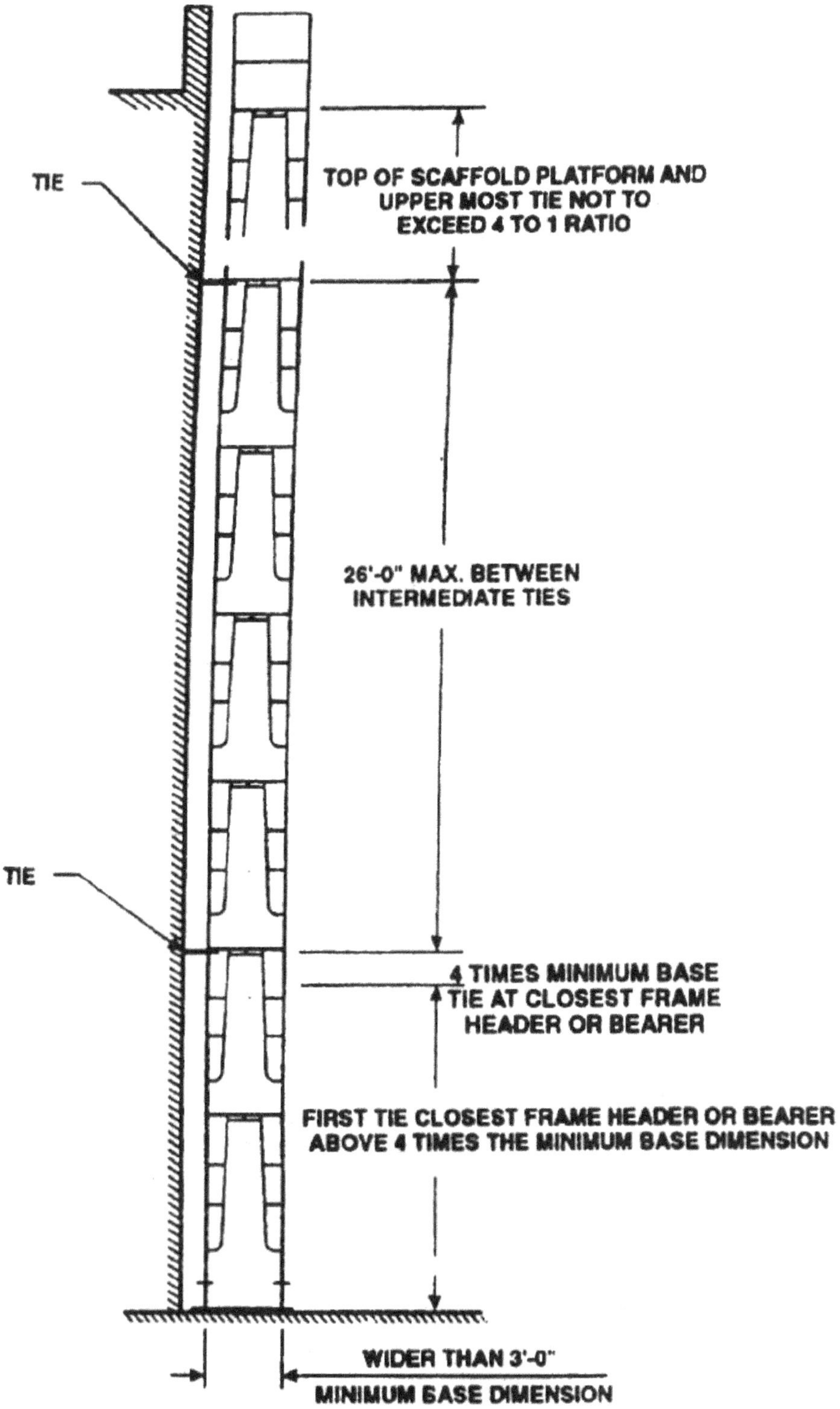

TIE

TOP OF SCAFFOLD PLATFORM AND
UPPER MOST TIE NOT TO
EXCEED 4 TO 1 RATIO

26'-0" MAX. BETWEEN
INTERMEDIATE TIES

TIE

4 TIMES MINIMUM BASE
TIE AT CLOSEST FRAME
HEADER OR BEARER

FIRST TIE CLOSEST FRAME HEADER OR BEARER
ABOVE 4 TIMES THE MINIMUM BASE DIMENSION

WIDER THAN 3'-0"

MINIMUM BASE DIMENSION

(Appendix E continued)

MAXIMUM VERTICAL TIE SPACING
3'- 0" AND NARROWER BASES

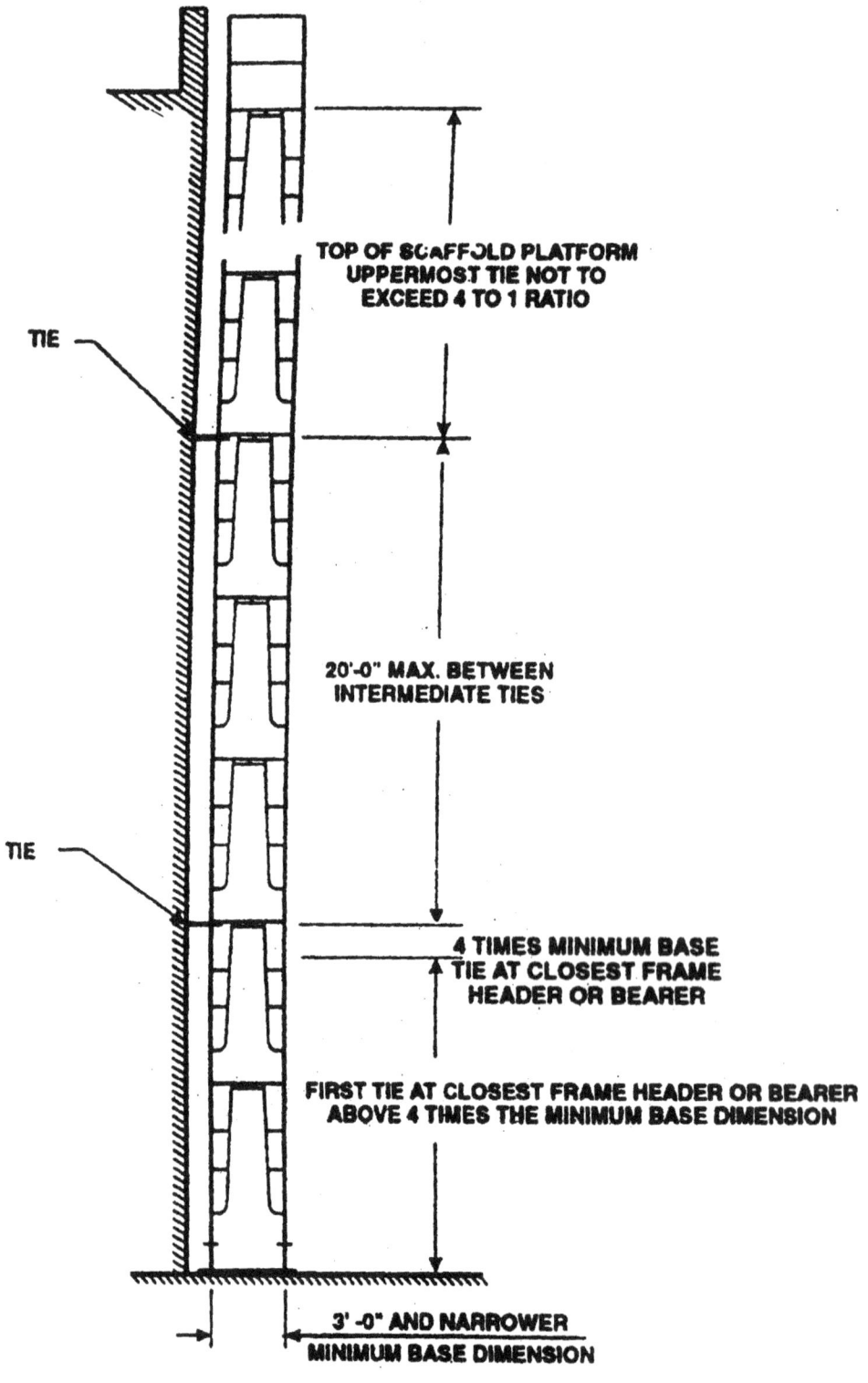

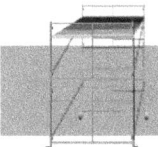

(Appendix E continued)

SYSTEM SCAFFOLD

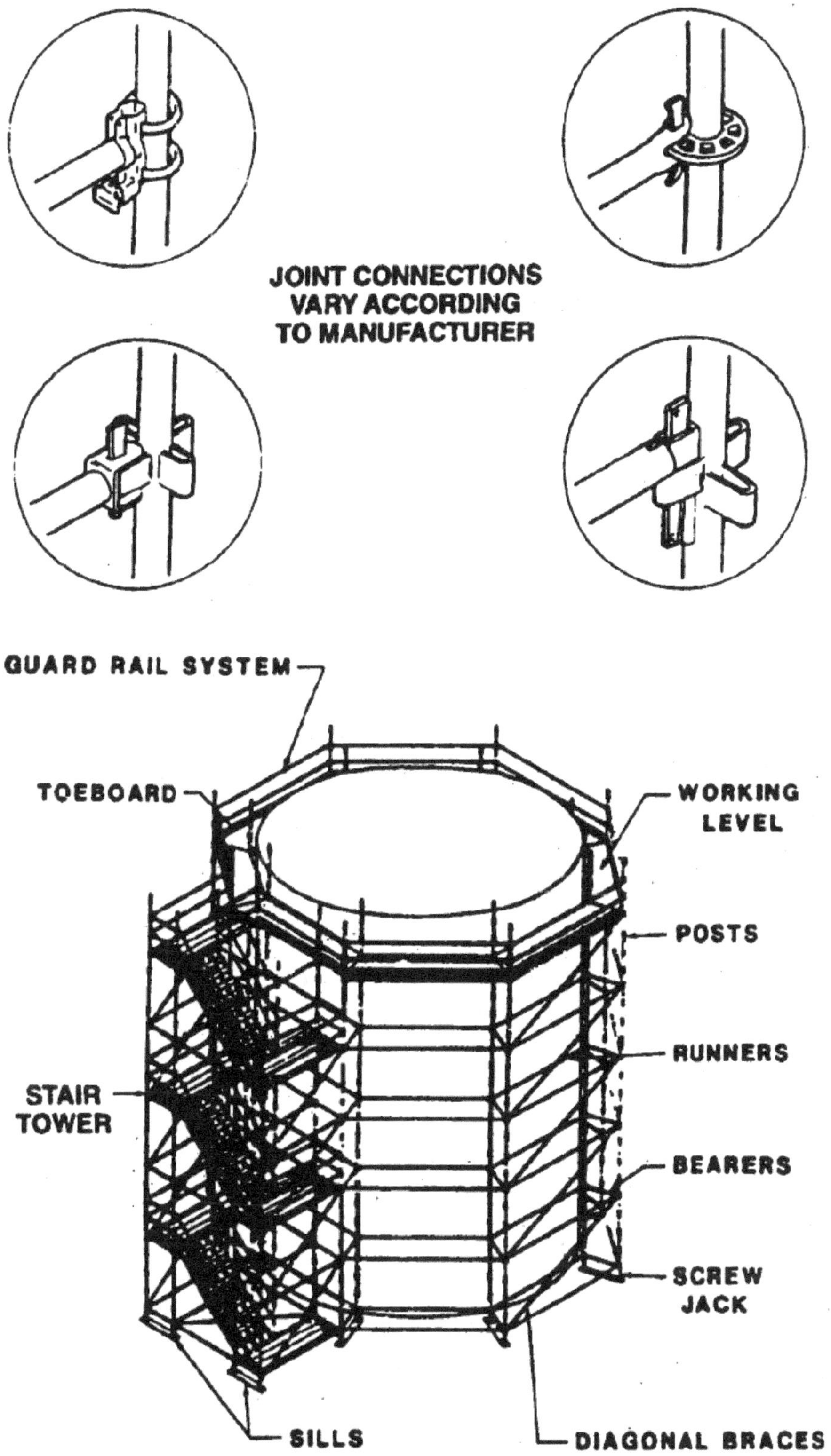

**JOINT CONNECTIONS
VARY ACCORDING
TO MANUFACTURER**

GUARD RAIL SYSTEM

TOEBOARD

WORKING LEVEL

POSTS

RUNNERS

STAIR TOWER

BEARERS

SCREW JACK

SILLS

DIAGONAL BRACES

(Appendix E continued)

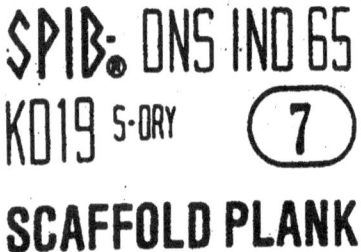

SCAFFOLD PLANK

Grade stamp courtesy of Southern Pine Inspection Bureau

Grade stamp courtesy of West Coast Lumber Inspection Bureau

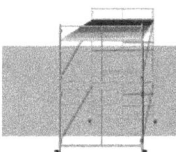

(Appendix E continued)

TUBE and COUPLER SCAFFOLD

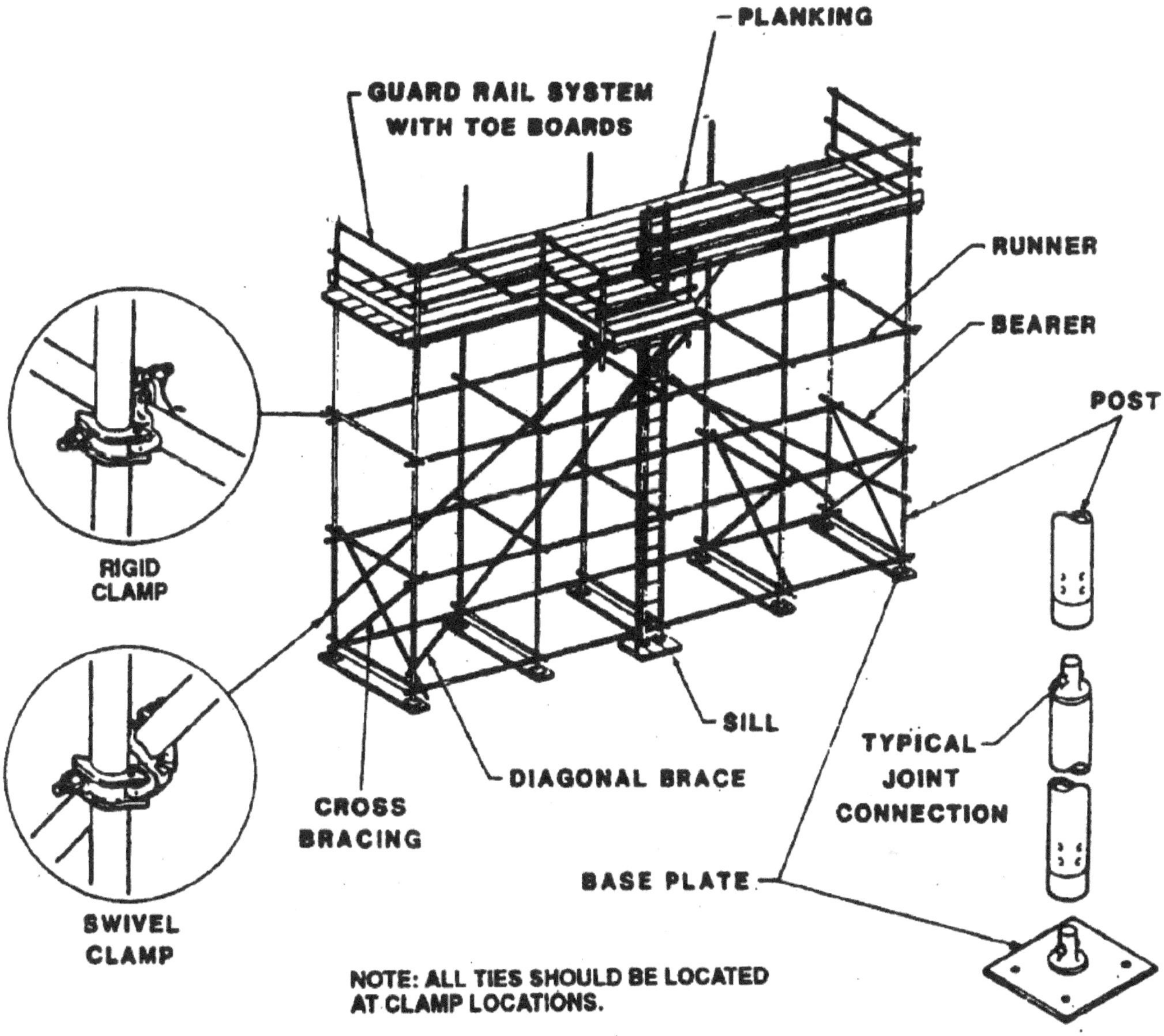

- PLANKING

GUARD RAIL SYSTEM
WITH TOE BOARDS

RUNNER

BEARER

POST

RIGID
CLAMP

SWIVEL
CLAMP

CROSS
BRACING

DIAGONAL BRACE

SILL

TYPICAL
JOINT
CONNECTION

BASE PLATE

NOTE: ALL TIES SHOULD BE LOCATED
AT CLAMP LOCATIONS.

(Appendix E continued)

SCAFFOLDING WORK SURFACES

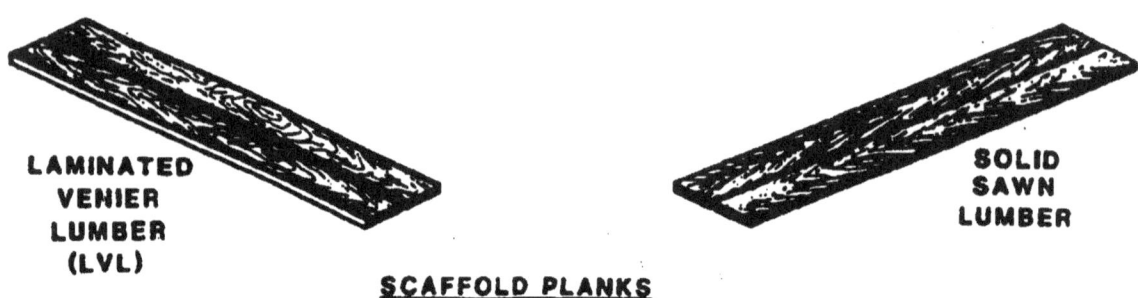

LAMINATED VENIER LUMBER (LVL)

SOLID SAWN LUMBER

SCAFFOLD PLANKS

FABRICATED SCAFFOLD DECK

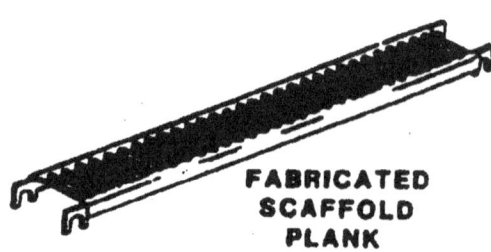

FABRICATED SCAFFOLD PLANK

DECORATOR PLANK

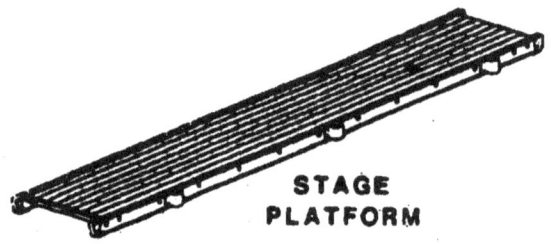

STAGE PLATFORM

WOOD SCAFFOLD PLATFORM

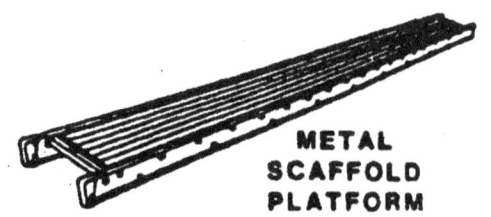

METAL SCAFFOLD PLATFORM

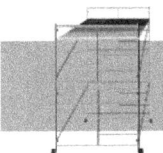

(Appendix E continued)

OUTRIGGER SCAFFOLD

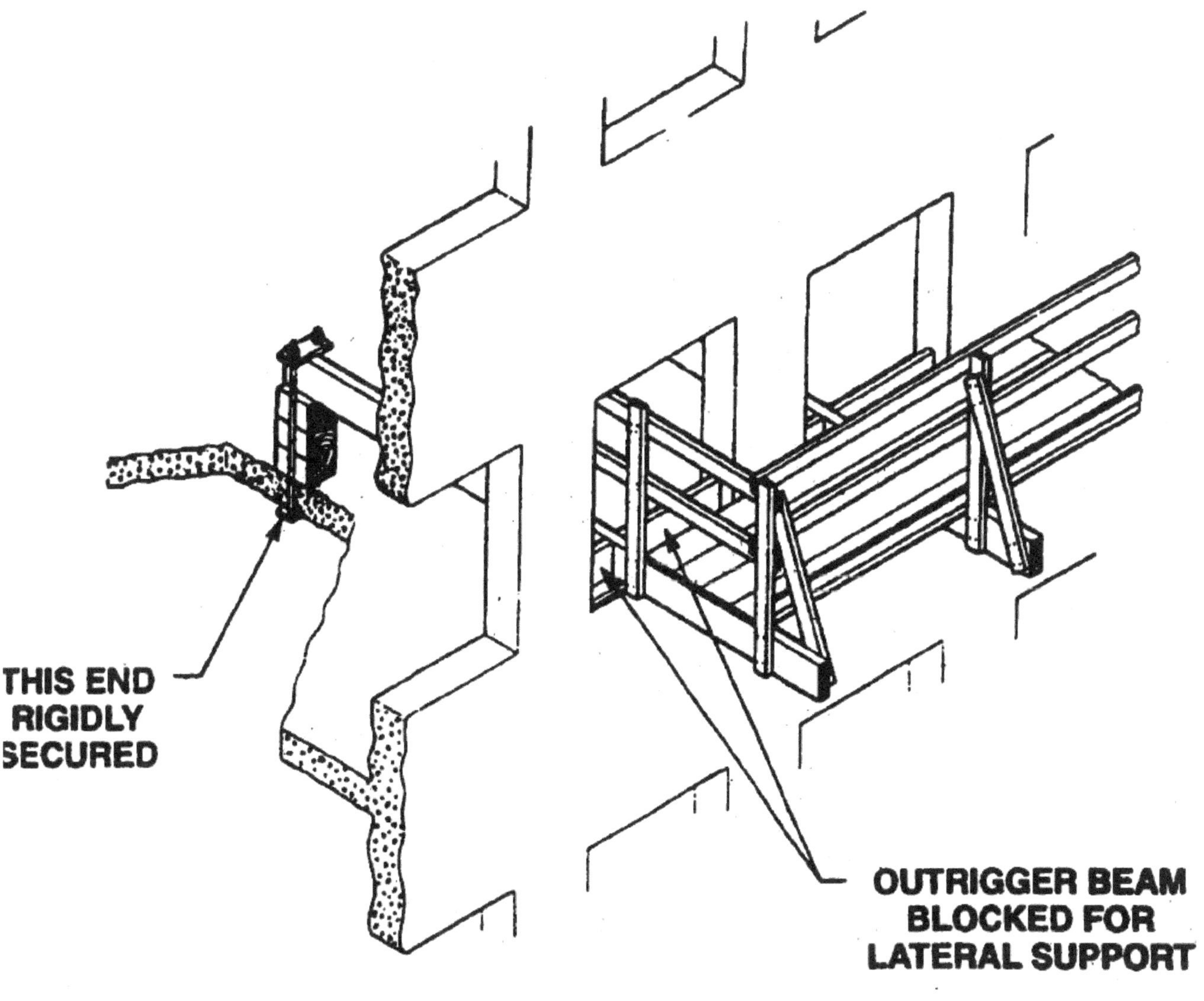

THIS END
RIGIDLY
SECURED

OUTRIGGER BEAM
BLOCKED FOR
LATERAL SUPPORT